"*Wʜᴀᴛ is that mutt—a rat-hound?*"

Now, one thing Father couldn't stand was to have anyone make fun of Mutt—and this fellow from New York was being downright insulting.

Without a word, he went into his office, brought out the shotgun he kept there, and cocked it. Mutt looked up, expectant but puzzled—it wasn't the hunting season and we weren't in the country. Father raised the empty gun to his shoulder. He cocked it, clicked the trigger, and said, "Bang—bang—go get 'em, boy."

Mutt was down the alley and around the corner in a flash. He was gone only two minutes, but it seemed a lot longer. Then he reappeared. We stared—and didn't believe what we saw.

Mutt was carrying a magnificent ruffed grouse—already stuffed and mounted!

The Dog Who Wouldn't Be

FARLEY MOWAT

The Dog Who Wouldn't Be

A NONPAREIL BOOK

David R. Godine, Publisher · Boston

Published in 2017 by
DAVID R. GODINE, *Publisher*
Boston, Massachusetts
www.godine.com

LIBRARY OF CONGRESS CATALOGING-IN-PUBLICATION DATA
Names: Mowat, Farley, author.
Title: The dog who wouldn't be / Farley Mowat.
Description: Jaffrey, New Hampshire : David R. Godine, Publisher, 2017. |
Originally published: Boston : Little, Brown, 1957. | Includes
bibliographical references and index.
Identifiers: LCCN 2017035911 | ISBN 9781567926125 (alk. paper)
Subjects: LCSH: Dogs.
Classification: LCC QL795.D6 M78 2017 | DDC 636.7—dc23
LC record available at https://lccn.loc.gov/2017035911

1970~2020
David R. Godine
⚬ Publisher ⚬
FIFTY YEARS

SEVENTH PRINTING, 2020
Printed in the United States of America

For my parents, who made the hours of my youth.
And for Mutt, who shared that time with me.

1

The Coming of Mutt

AN OPPRESSIVE darkness shadowed the city of Saskatoon on an August day in 1929. By the clock it was hardly noon. By the sun— but the earth had obliterated the sun. Rising in the new deserts of the southwest, and lifting high on autumnal winds, the desecrated soil of the prairies drifted northward; and the sky grew dark.

In our small house on the outskirts of the city my mother switched on the electric lights and continued with the task of preparing luncheon for my father and for me. Father had not yet returned from his office, nor I from school. Mother was alone with the somber day.

The sound of the doorbell brought her unwillingly from the kitchen into the hall. She opened the front door no more than a few inches, as if expecting the menace of the sky to thrust its way past her into the house.

There was no menace in the appearance of the visitor who waited apologetically on the step. A small boy, perhaps ten years of age, stood shuffling his feet in the gray grit that had been falling soundlessly across the city for a day and a night. He held a wicker basket before him and, as the door opened, he swung the basket forward and spoke in a voice that was husky with the dust and with the expectation of rebuff.

"Missus," he asked in a pale, high tone, "would you want to buy a duck?"

Mother was a bit nonplussed by this odd echo of a catch phrase that had already withered and staled in the mouths of the comedians of the era. Nevertheless, she looked into the basket and to her astonishment beheld three emaciated ducklings, their bills gaping in the heat, and, wedged between them, a nondescript and bedraggled pup.

She was touched, and curious—although she certainly did not want to buy a duck.

"I don't think so," she said kindly. "Why are you selling them?"

The boy took courage and returned her smile.

"I gotta," he said. "The slough out to the farm is dry. We ate the big ducks, but these were too small to eat. I sold some down to the Chinee Grill. You want the rest, lady? They're cheap—only a dime each."

"I'm sorry," Mother replied. "I've no place to keep a duck. But where did you get the little dog?"

The boy shrugged his shoulders. "Oh, *him*," he said without much interest. "He was kind of an accident, you might say. I guess somebody dumped him out of a car right by our gate. I brung him with me in case. But dogs is hard to sell." He brightened up a little as an idea struck him. "Say, lady, you want him? I'll sell him for a nickel—that way you'll *save* a nickel for yourself."

The Coming of Mutt

Mother hesitated. Then almost involuntarily her hand went to the basket. The pup was thirsty beyond thirst, and those outstretched fingers must have seemed to him as fountains straight from heaven. He clambered hastily over the ducks and grabbed.

The boy was quick to sense his advantage and to press it home.

"He likes you, lady, see? He's yours for just *four* cents!"

Less than a month had elapsed since my parents and I had come out of the verdant depths of southern Ontario into the arid and dust-shrouded prairies.

It had seemed a foolhardy venture then, for those were the beginnings of the hard times, even in the east; while in the west the hard times—the times of drought and failure—were already old. I do not know what possessed my father to make him exchange the security of his job in Windsor for a most uncertain future as Saskatoon's librarian. It may be that the name itself, Saskatoon, Saskatchewan, attracted him irresistibly. It may have been simply that he was tired of the physical and mental confines of a province grown staid and stolid in its years.

In any case he made his decision in the fall of 1928, and the rest of us acquiesced in it; I, with a high heart and bright anticipation; Mother, with grave reservations and gloomy prophecies.

Father spent that winter building a caravan, a trailer-house which was destined to carry us westward. It was a long winter for me. On Saturdays I joined my father under a shed and here we hammered and sawed industriously, and the caravan took shape. It was an unconventional shape, for my father was a sailor at heart and he had had but little experience in the design of land conveyances. Our caravan was, in reality, a houseboat perched precariously on the four thin wheels of an old Model T chassis. Her aspect was bluff and uncompromising. Her sides towered straight from the frame a full seven feet to a gently cambered deck (which was never referred to as a roof). She was big-boned and buxom, and she dwarfed poor Eardlie—our Model A Ford convertible—as a floating derrick dwarfs the tug which tows it.

Some of Father's friends used to come by now and again to watch our progress. They never said much, but when they went away it was with much thoughtful shakings of their heads.

Perhaps our caravan was no thing of beauty, but she was at least a thing of comfort. My father was an ingenious builder and he had fitted her cabin with every nautical convenience. There was a compact galley with a primus stove on gimbals, gimbaled lamps, great quantities of locker space, stowage for charts, a Seth Thomas chronometer on the forward bulkhead, two luxurious berths for my parents, and a folding pipe-berth for me. Dishes, our many books, and other loose oddments were neatly and securely racked in fitted cupboards so that even in the wildest weather they could not come adrift.

It was as well that my father took such pains to make the interior seaworthy, for, as we headed westward, we discovered that our wheeled vessel was—as sailors say—more than somewhat crank. Slab-sided and immense, she was the prey of every wind that blew. When a breeze took her from the flank she would sway heavily and, as like as not, scuttle ponderously to the wrong side of the road, pushing poor Eardlie with her. A head wind would force Eardlie into second gear and even then he would have to strain and boil furiously to keep headway on his balky charge. A stern wind was almost as bad, for then the great bulk of the tow would try to override the little car and, failing in this, would push Eardlie forward at speeds which chilled my mother's heart.

All in all it was a memorable journey for an eight-year-old boy. I had my choice of riding in Eardlie's rumble seat, where I became the gunner in a Sopwith Camel; or I could ride in the caravan itself and pilot my self-contained rocket into outer space. I preferred the caravan, for it was a private world and a brave one. My folding bunk-bed was placed high up under the rear window, and here I could lie—carefully strapped into place against the effect of negative gravity (and high winds)—and guide my spaceship through the void to those far planets known as Ohio, Minnesota, Wisconsin, Michigan, and North Dakota.

When we re-entered Canada at the little town of Estevan, I no longer needed to exercise my imagination by conjuring up otherwordly landscapes. The desolation of the southeast corner of Saskatchewan was appalling, and it was terrifyingly real. The dust storms had been at work there for several years and they had left behind them an incipient desert. Here and there the whitening bones of abandoned buildings remained to mark the death of hopes; and the wind-burnished wood of engulfed fences protruded from the drifts of subsoil that were overwhelming the works of man.

We were all subdued. Although my father tried hard to reassure us, saying that things would improve as we went north, I can remember no great improvement in that lunar landscape as we passed through endless little hamlets that appeared to be in the last stages of dry rot, and as we traversed the burning expanses of drought-stricken fields.

Mother was openly mutinous by the time we reached Saskatoon and even my father was a little depressed. But I was at an age when tragedy has no permanent reality. I saw only that here was a land foreign to all my imaginings, and one that offered limitless possibilities for totally new kinds of adventures. I was fascinated by the cracked white saucers that were the dried-up sloughs; by the dusty clusters of poplar trees that, for some reason which still escapes me, were known as bluffs; and by a horizon that was limitless. I well remember the words of an old man at whose farm we stopped to get some water for Eardlie's heated radiator.

"She's flat, boy," he told me. "This country's flat enough so's you stand on a gopher hill you can see nigh off to China." I believed him, and I still do—for, geographers to the contrary, there is no limit to man's vision on those broad plains.

The innumerable little gophers roused my speculative interest, as did the bitter alkaline waters of the few remaining wells, the great soaring shapes of the hawks that rose from the fence posts by the roadsides, and the quaver of coyotes in the evening that sent a shiver down my back. Even Saskatoon, when we found it at last sprawled in exhausted despair beside the trickle of the river, was pregnant with adventure. Founded not more than three decades earlier, as a tiny temperance outpost of the Methodist faith, it had outgrown its natal influences and had become a city of thirty thousand people who embraced the beliefs and customs of half the countries of the Western world. Many of these, particularly the Dukhobors, Mennonites, and Hutterites, were mystery distilled in the eyes of an eight-year-old from the staid Anglo-Saxon province of Ontario.

Father rented a house for us in the northern sections of the city and this jerry-built little box, which was an incinerator in summer and a polar outpost in the winter, became my home. To me it seemed admirable, for it was close to the outskirts of the city—and having been so recently grafted on the face of the plains, Saskatoon had as yet no outer ring of suburbs. You had but to step off the streetcar at the end of the last row of houses, and you were on virgin prairie. The transition in space and time was abrupt and complete and I could make that transition not only on Saturdays, but on any afternoon when school was over.

If there was one drawback to the new life in Saskatoon, it was that we had no dog. During my lifetime we had owned, or had been owned by, a steady succession of dogs. As a newborn baby I had been guarded by a Border collie named Sapper who was one day doused with boiling water by a vicious neighbor, and who went insane as a result. But there had always been other dogs during my first eight years, until we moved to the west and became, for the moment, dogless. The prairies could be only half real to a boy without a dog.

I began agitating for one almost as soon as we arrived and I found a willing ally in my father—though his motives were not mine.

The Dog Who Wouldn't Be

For many years he had been exposed to the colorful tales of my Great-uncle Frank, who homesteaded in Alberta in 1900. Frank was a hunter born, and most of his stories dealt with the superlative shooting to be had on the western plains. Before we were properly settled in Saskatoon my father determined to test those tales. He bought a fine English shotgun, a shooting coat, cases of ammunition, a copy of the *Saskatchewan Game Laws*, and a handbook on shotgun shooting. There remained only one indispensable item—a hunting dog.

One evening he arrived home from the library with such a beast in tow behind him. Its name was Crown Prince Challenge Indefatigable. It stood about as high as the dining-room table and, as far as Mother and I could judge, consisted mainly of feet and tongue. Father was annoyed at our levity and haughtily informed us that the Crown Prince was an Irish setter, kennel bred and field trained, and a dog to delight the heart of any expert. We remained unimpressed. Purebred he may have been, and the possessor of innumerable cups and ribbons, but to my eyes he seemed a singularly useless sort of beast with but one redeeming feature. I greatly admired the way he drooled. I have never known a dog who could drool as the Crown Prince could. He never stopped, except to flop his way to the kitchen sink and tank-up on water. He left a wet and sticky trail wherever he went. He had little else to recommend him, for he was moronic.

Mother might have overlooked his obvious defects, had it not been for his price. She could not overlook that, for the owner was asking two hundred dollars, and we could no more afford such a sum than we could have afforded a Cadillac. Crown Prince left the next morning, but Father was not discouraged, and it was clear that he would try again.

My parents had been married long enough to achieve that delicate balance of power which enables a married couple to endure each other. They were both adept in the evasive tactics of marital politics—but Mother was a little more adept.

She realized that a dog was now inevitable, and when chance brought the duck boy—as we afterwards referred to him—to our door on that dusty August day, Mother showed her mettle by snatching the initiative right out of my father's hands.

By buying the duck boy's pup, she not only placed herself in a position to forestall the purchase of an expensive dog of my father's choice but she was also able to save six cents in cash. She was never one to despise a bargain.

When I came home from school the bargain was installed in a soap carton in the kitchen. He looked to be a somewhat dubious buy at any price. Small, emaciated, and caked liberally with cow manure, he peered up at me in a nearsighted sort of way. But when I knelt beside him and extended an exploratory hand he roused himself and sank his puppy teeth into my thumb with such satisfactory gusto that my doubts dissolved. I knew that he and I would get along.

My father's reaction was of a different kind.

He arrived home at six o'clock that night and he was hardly in the door before he began singing the praises of a springer-spaniel bitch he had just seen. He seemed hardly even to hear at first when

Mother interrupted to remark that we already had a dog, and that two would be too many.

When he beheld the pup he was outraged; but the ambush had been well and truly laid and before he could recover himself, Mother unmasked her guns.

"Isn't he *lovely*, darling?" she asked sweetly. "And so *cheap*. Do you know, I've actually saved you a hundred and ninety-nine dollars and ninety-six cents? Enough to pay for all your ammunition and for that *expensive* new gun you bought."

My father was game, and he rallied quickly. He pointed scornfully at the pup, and in a voice sharp with exasperation he replied:

"But, damn it all—that—that 'thing' isn't a *hunting* dog!"

Mother was ready for him. "How do you *know*, dear," she asked mildly, "until you've tried him out?"

There could be no adequate reply to this. It was as impossible to predict what the pup might grow up to be, as it was to deduce what his ancestry might have been. Father turned to me for support, but I would not meet his eye, and he knew then that he had been out-maneuvered.

He accepted defeat with his usual good grace. I can clearly remember, and with awe, what he had to say to some friends who dropped in for a drink not three evenings later. The pup, relatively clean, and already beginning to fatten out a little, was presented to the guests.

"He's imported," Father explained in a modest tone of voice. "I understand he's the only one of his kind in the west. A Prince Albert retriever, you know. Marvelous breed for upland shooting."

The Coming of Mutt

Unwilling to confess their ignorance, the guests looked vaguely knowing. "What do you call him?" one of them asked.

I put my foot in it then. Before my father could reply, I forestalled him.

"*I* call him Mutt," I said. And I was appalled by the look my father gave me.

He turned his back on me and smiled confidentially at the guests.

"You have to be rather careful with these highly bred specimens," he explained, "it doesn't always do to let them know their kennel names. Better to give them a simple bourgeois name like Sport, or Nipper, or—" and he gagged a trifle—"or even Mutt."

2

Early Days

DURING his first few weeks with us Mutt astonished us all by his maturity of outlook. He never really was a puppy, at least not after he came to us. Perhaps the ordeal with the ducks had aged him prematurely; perhaps he was simply born adult in mind. In any case he resolutely eschewed the usual antics of puppyhood. He left behind him no mangled slippers, no torn upholstery, and no stains upon the rugs. He did not wage mock warfare with people's bare feet, nor did he make the night hideous when he was left to spend the dark hours alone in the kitchen. There was about him, from the first day he came to us, an aura of resolution and restraint, and dignity. He took life seriously, and he expected us to do likewise.

Nor was he malleable. His character was immutably resolved before we ever knew him and, throughout his life, it did not change.

I suspect that at some early moment of his existence he concluded there was no future in being a dog. And so, with the tenacity which marked his every act, he set himself to become something else. Subconsciously he no longer believed that he was a dog at all, yet he did not feel, as so many foolish canines appear to do, that he was human. He was tolerant of both species, but he claimed kin to neither.

If he was unique in attitude, he was also unique in his appearance. In size he was not far from a setter, but in all other respects he was very far from any known breed. His hindquarters were elevated several inches higher than his forequarters; and at the same time he was distinctly canted from left to right. The result was that, when he was approaching, he appeared to be drifting off about three points to starboard, while simultaneously giving an eerie impression of a submarine starting on a crash dive. It was impossible to tell, unless you knew him very well indeed, exactly where he was heading, or what his immediate objective might be. His eyes gave no clue, for they were so close-set that he looked to be, and may have been, somewhat cross-eyed. The total illusion had its practical advantages, for gophers and cats pursued by Mutt could seldom decide where he was aiming until they discovered, too late, that he was actually on a collision course with them.

An even more disquieting physical characteristic was the fact that his hind legs moved at a slower speed than did his front ones. This was theoretically explicable on the grounds that his hind legs were much longer than his forelegs—but an understanding of this explanation could not dispel the unsettling impression that Mutt's forward section was slowly and relentlessly pulling away from the tardy after-end.

Early Days

And yet, despite all this, Mutt was not unprepossessing in general appearance. He had a handsome black and white coat of fine, almost silky hair, with exceptionally long "feathers" on his legs. His tail was long, limber, and expressive. Although his ears were rather large and limp, his head was broad and high-domed. A black mask covered all of his face except for his bulbous nose, which was pure white. He was not really handsome, yet he possessed the same sort of dignified grotesquerie which so distinguished Abraham Lincoln and the Duke of Wellington.

He also possessed a peculiar savoir-faire that had a disconcerting effect upon strangers. So strong was Mutt's belief that he was not simply "dog" that he was somehow able to convey this conviction to human onlookers.

One bitterly cold day in January Mother went down-town to do some post-Christmas shopping and Mutt accompanied her. She parted from him outside the Hudson Bay Department Store, for Mutt had strong antipathies, even in those early months, and one of these was directed against the famous Company of Gentlemen Adventurers. Mother was inside the store for almost an hour, while Mutt was left to shiver on the wind-swept pavement.

When Mother emerged at last, Mutt had forgotten that he had voluntarily elected to remain outside. Instead he was nursing a grievance at what seemed to him to be a calculated indifference to his comfort on my mother's part. He had decided to sulk, and when he sulked he became intractable. Nothing that Mother would say could persuade him to get up off the frigid concrete and accompany her home. Mother pleaded. Mutt ignored her and fixed his gaze upon the steamed-up windows of the Star Café across the street.

Neither of them was aware of the small audience which had formed around them. There were three Dukhobors in their quaint winter costumes, a policeman enveloped in a buffalo-skin coat, and a dentist from the nearby Medical Arts Building. Despite the cold, these strangers stood and watched with growing fascination as Mother ordered and Mutt, with slightly lifted lip and *sotto-voce* mutters, adamantly refused to heed. Both of them were becoming exasperated, and the tone of their utterances grew increasingly vehement.

It was at this point that the dentist lost touch with reality. He stepped forward and addressed Mutt in man-to-man tones.

"Oh, I say, old boy, be reasonable!" he said reproachfully.

Mutt replied with a murmur of guttural disdain, and this was too much for the policeman.

"What seems to be the matter here?" he asked.

Mother explained. "He won't go home. He just won't go!"

The policeman was a man of action. He wagged his mittened paw under Mutt's nose. "Can't you see the lady's cold?" he asked sternly.

Mutt rolled his eyes and yawned and the policeman lost his temper. "Now, see here," he cried, "you just move along or, by the gods, I'll run you in!"

It was fortunate that my father and Eardlie came by at this moment. Father had seen Mutt and Mother in arguments before, and he acted with dispatch, picking them both up almost bodily and pushing them into Eardlie's front seat. He did not linger, for he had no desire to be a witness to the reactions of the big policeman and of the dentist when they became aware of the fact that they had been arguing with a dog upon a public street.

Arguments with Mutt were almost invariably fruitless. As he grew older he became more vocal and more argumentative. When he was asked to do something which did not please him he would begin to mutter. If he was pressed, the muttering would grow in volume, rising and falling in pitch. It was not a growl nor was it in the least threatening. It was a stubborn bumbling sound, quite indescribable.

It happened that Father was writing a novel that first winter in the west, and he was extremely touchy about being disturbed while working on it.

One evening he was hunched over his portable typewriter in the living room, his face drawn and haggard with concentration, but he was getting very little actually down on paper. Mother and I, recognizing the symptoms, had discreetly retired to the kitchen, but Mutt had remained in the living room, asleep before the open fire.

Mutt was not a silent sleeper. He snored with a peculiar penetrating sound and, being a dog who dreamed actively, his snores were often punctuated by high-pitched yelps as he galloped across the dream prairie in pursuit of a rabbit.

He must have been lucky that evening. Perhaps it was an old and infirm rabbit he was chasing, or perhaps the rabbit slipped and fell. At any rate Mutt closed with it, and instantly the living room reverberated to a horrendous conflict.

The Dog Who Wouldn't Be

Father, blasted so violently from his creative mood, was enraged. He roared at Mutt, who, awakened harshly in the very moment of victory, was inclined to be surly about the interruption.

"Get out, you insufferable beast!" Father yelled at him.

Mutt curled his lip and prepared to argue.

Father was now almost beside himself. "I said *out*—you animated threshing machine!"

Mutt's argumentative mutters immediately rose in volume. Mother and I shivered slightly and stared at each other with dreadful surmise.

Our apprehensions were justified by the sound of shattering glass, as a volume of *Everyman's Encyclopedia* banged against the dining-room wall, on the wrong side of the French doors. Mutt appeared in the kitchen at almost the same instant. Without so much as a look at us, he thumped down the basement stairs—his whole attitude radiating outrage.

Father was immediately contrite. He followed Mutt down into the cellar, and we could hear him apologizing—but it did no good. Mutt would not deign to notice him for three days. Physical violence in lieu of argument was, to Mutt, a cardinal sin.

He had another exasperating habit that he developed very early in life, and never forgot. When it was manifestly impossible for him to avoid some unpleasant duty by means of argument, he would feign deafness. On occasions I lost my temper and, bending down so that I could lift one of his long ears, would scream my orders at him in the voice of a Valkyrie. But Mutt would simply turn his face toward me with a bland and interrogative look that seemed to say with insufferable mildness, "I'm sorry—did you speak?"

We could not take really effective steps to cure him of this irritating habit, for it was one he shared with my paternal grandfather, who sometimes visited us. Grandfather was stone deaf to anything that involved effort on his part, yet he could hear, and respond to, the word "whiskey" if it was whispered inside a locked bedroom three floors above the chair in which he habitually sat.

It will be clear by now that Mutt was not an easy dog to live with. Yet the intransigence which made it so difficult to cope with him made it even more difficult—and at times well-nigh impossible—for him to cope with the world in general. His stubbornness marked him out for a tragicomic role throughout his life. But Mutt's struggles with a perverse fate were not, unfortunately, his alone. He involved those about him, inevitably and often catastrophically, in his confused battle with life.

Wherever he went he left deep-etched memories that were alternately vivid with the screaming hues of outrage, or cloudy with the muddy colors of near dementia. He carried with him the aura of a Don Quixote and it was in that atmosphere that my family and I lived for more than a decade.

3

The Blues

PROBABLY THE greatest indignity which Mutt ever experienced at our hands came about as a result of my father's feeling for the English language. As a librarian, an author, and as a well-read man, he was a militant defender of the sanctity of the written and the spoken word, and when he encountered words that were being ill used, his anger knew no bounds.

North Americans being what they are, my father was often roused to fury. I have seen him turn his back upon one of the new nobles of our times—a prominent man of business—simply because the poor fellow remarked that he was about to immediatize the crafting of a new product. Father believed that this sort of jabberwocky was inexcusable, but what really irritated him beyond measure was the jargon of the advertising writers.

He felt so strongly about this that popular magazines were seldom allowed to enter our home. This was something of a hardship for Mother, but it was as nothing to the hardships both she and I suffered if, by mischance, my father found a copy of the *Woman's Boon Companion* hidden under the cushions of the living-room couch. With the offending magazine in his hand, my father would take the floor and subject his captive audience to concentrated and vitriolic comment on the future facing a world that allowed such sabotage of all that he held dear.

These incidents were fortunately rare, yet they occurred from time to time when one of us grew careless. It was as the result of one such incident that Mutt came to suffer the blues.

It began on a spring evening in the second year of Mutt's life. Mother had had visitors for tea that afternoon, and one of the ladies had brought with her a copy of a famous woman's magazine which she neglected to take away again.

My father was restless that evening. He had forgotten to bring the usual armful of books home from the library. The mosquitoes were too avid to allow him to indulge in his favorite evening pastime of stalking dandelions in the back yard. He stayed in the house, pacing aimlessly about the living room until my mother could stand it no longer.

"For Heaven's sake, stop prowling," she said at last. "Sit down and read a magazine—there's one behind my chair."

She must have been completely preoccupied with her knitting when she spoke. It was seldom that my mother was so obtuse.

In my bedroom, where I was writing an essay on Champlain, I vaguely heard but did not heed her words. Mutt, asleep and dreaming at my feet, heard nothing. Neither of us was prepared for the anguished cry that rang through the house a few moments later. My father's voice was noted for its parade-ground quality even when, as in this case, the words themselves seemed quite inscrutable.

The Blues

"What the devil *do* the neighbors say when they see your dirty underwear?" he thundered.

Mutt woke so suddenly that he banged his head painfully against my desk. Champlain vanished from my thoughts, and I wracked my mind frantically for memories of guilty deeds connected with underwear. Then we heard mother's voice, soothing and quiet, dispelling the echoes of the blast. My heartbeat returned to normal and my curiosity led me out into the hall to peer through the living-room door.

My father was pacing again, with a sergeant major's tread. He was waving an open magazine in front of him and I caught a glimpse of a full-color, full-page advertisement which depicted an unspeakably dirty pair of drawers swinging like a flag of ill fame from a clothes-line. Running across the page in broad crimson letters was the mortifying accusation:

THESE MAY BE YOURS!

Mother was sitting quietly in her chair, but her lips were pursed. "Really, Angus!" she was saying. "*Control* yourself! After all, everyone has to live, and if that company can't sell its bluing, how can *it* live?"

My father replied with a pungent, and what I took to be an appropriate, suggestion, but Mother ignored him.

"Perhaps it *is* a trifle vulgar," she continued, "but it's just intended to catch the reader's attention; and it does, doesn't it?"

There could be no doubt that it had caught my father's attention.

"Well, then," Mother concluded triumphantly, "you see?" It was the phrase with which she always clinched her arguments.

The magazine was quietly consigned to the incinerator the next morning, and Mother and I assumed that this particular storm had blown over. We were in error, but neither of us had much knowledge of the working of the subconscious. We never guessed that the incident was still festering in some deep and hidden recess of my father's mind.

Summer drew on and the sloughs again grew dry and white; the young grain wizened and burned, and another season of drought was upon us. A film of dust hung continuously in the scorching air and we were never free of the gritty touch of it, except when we stripped off our clothing and went to soak in the bathtub. For Mutt there was no such relief. His long coat caught and trapped the dust until the hair became matted and discolored, assuming a jaundiced saffron hue, but he would not, in those early days, voluntarily turn to water to escape his misery.

He was a true son of the drought. I suppose that he had seen so little water in his first months of life that he had a right to be suspicious of it. At any rate he shied away from water in any quantity, as a cayoose shies from a rattlesnake. When we decided to force a bath upon him, he not only became argumentative and deaf, but if he could escape us, he would crawl under the garage floor, where he would remain without food or drink until we gave in and solemnly assured him that the bath was off.

Not the least difficult part of the bath was the devising of a plan whereby Mutt might be lured, all unsuspecting, into the basement

The Blues

where the laundry tubs stood waiting. This problem required a different solution each time, for Mutt had a long memory, and his bath suspicions were easily aroused. On one occasion we released a live gopher in the cellar and then, encountering it "unexpectedly," called upon Mutt to slay it. This worked once.

The bath itself was a severe ordeal to all who were involved. During the earlier attempts we wore raincoats, sou'westers, and rubber boots, but we found these inadequate. Later we wore only simple breechclouts. Mutt never gave up, and he would sometimes go to incredible lengths to cheat the tub. Once he snatched a piece of naphtha soap out of my hand and swallowed it, whether accidentally or not I do not know. He began frothing almost immediately, and we curtailed the bath and called the veterinary.

The veterinary was a middle-aged and unimaginative man whose practice was largely limited to healing boils on horses and hard udders on cows. He refused to believe that Mutt had voluntarily swallowed soap, and he left in something of a huff. Mutt took advantage of the hullabaloo to vanish. He returned twenty-four hours later looking pale and emaciated—having proved the emetic efficacy of naphtha soap beyond all question.

The decision to bathe Mutt was never lightly made, and we tended to postpone it as long as possible. He was long overdue for a cleansing when, in late July, I went away to spend a few days at a friend's cottage on Lake Manitou.

I enjoyed myself at Manitou, which is one of the saltiest of the west's salt sloughs. My friend and I spent most of our days trying to swim, despite the fact that the saline content of the water was so high that it was impossible to sink deep enough to reach a point of balance. We slithered about on the surface, acquiring painful sunburns and bad cases of salt-water itch.

I was in a carefree and happy mood when, on Monday morning, I arrived back in Saskatoon. I came up the front walk of our house whistling for Mutt and bearing a present for him—a dead gopher that we had picked up on the road home. He did not respond to my whistle. A little uneasily I pushed through the front door and found Mother sitting on the chesterfield, looking deeply distressed. She stood up when she saw me and clutched me to her bosom.

"Oh, darling," she cried, "your poor, *poor* dog! Oh, your *poor*, poor dog!"

A lethal apprehension overwhelmed me. I stiffened in her arms. "What's the matter with him?" I demanded.

Mother released me and looked into my eyes. "Be brave, darling," she said. "You'd better see him for yourself. He's under the garage."

I was already on my way.

Mutt's grotto under the garage was his private sanctuary, and it could be reached only through a narrow burrow. I got down on my hands and knees and peered into the gloom. As my eyes became accustomed to the darkness, I could discern a vague but Muttlike shape. He was curled up in the farthest recess, his head half hidden by his tail, but with one eye exposed and glaring balefully out of the murk. He did not seem to be seriously damaged and I ordered him to emerge.

The Blues

He did not move.

In the end I had to crawl into the burrow, grasp him firmly by the tail, and drag him out by brute force. And then I was so startled by his appearance that I released my grip and he scuttled back to cover.

Mutt was no longer a black and white dog, or even a black and yellow one. He was a vivid black and blue. Those sections of his coat that had once been white were now of an unearthly ultramarine shade. The effect was ghastly, particularly about the head, for even his nose and muzzle were bright blue.

Mutt's transformation had taken place the day I left for Manitou. He was indignant and annoyed that he had been left behind, and for the rest of that day he sulked. When no one gave him the sympathy he felt was due him, he left the house, and he did not return home until evening. His return was notable.

Somewhere out on the broad prairie to the east of town he found the means with which to revenge himself upon humanity. He found a dead horse in that most satisfactory state of decomposition which best lends itself to being rolled upon. Mutt rolled with diligence.

He arrived home at a little after nine o'clock, and no doubt he trusted to the dusk to conceal him until he could reach his grotto. He was caught unawares when father leaped upon him from ambush. He made a frantic effort to escape and succeeded briefly, only to be trapped in the back yard. Squalling bitterly, he was at last dragged into the basement. The doors were closed and locked and the laundry tubs were filled.

The Dog Who Wouldn't Be

Father has never been willing to describe in any detail the events that followed, but Mother—although she did not actually descend into the basement herself—was able to give me a reasonably circumstantial account. It must have been an epic struggle. It lasted almost three hours and the sounds and smells of battle reached Mother, via the hot-air registers, without appreciable diminution. She told me that both my father and Mutt had become hoarse and silent by the end of the second hour, but that the sounds of water sluicing violently back and forth over the basement floor testified clearly that the struggle was not yet at an end.

It was nearly midnight before Father appeared alone at the head of the cellar stairs. He was stripped to the buff, and close to exhaustion. After a stiff drink and a bath of his own, he went to bed without so much as hinting to Mother of the dreadful things that had happened on the dank battleground downstairs.

Mutt spent the balance of the night outside, under the front porch. He was evidently too fatigued even to give vent to his vexation by an immediate return to the dead horse—although he probably had this in mind for the morrow.

But when dawn came, not even the lure of the horse was sufficient to make him forgo his usual morning routine.

It had long been his unvarying habit to spend the hours between dawn and breakfast time going his rounds through the back alleys in the neighborhood. He had a regular route, and he seldom deviated from it. There were certain garbage cans that he never missed, and there were, of course, a number of important telephone poles that had to be attended to. His path used to take him down the alleyway between Ninth and Tenth Avenues, thence to the head of the New Bridge, and finally to the rear premises of the restaurants and grocery stores in the neighborhood of the Five Corners. Returning home, he would proceed along the main thoroughfare, inspecting fireplugs en route. By the time he started home, there would usually be a good number of people on the streets, bound across the river to their places of work. Mutt had no intimation of disaster on this particular morning until he joined the throng of south-bound workers.

Mother had no warning either until, at a quarter to eight, the telephone rang. Mother answered it and an irate female voice shouted in her ear, "You people should be put in jail! You'll see if it's so funny when I put the law onto you!" The receiver at the other end went down with a crash, and Mother went back to making breakfast. She was always phlegmatic in the early hours, and she assumed that this threatening tirade was simply the result of a wrong number. She actually smiled as she told Father about it over the breakfast table. She was still smiling when the police arrived.

There were two constables, and they were pleasant and polite when Mother answered the door. One of them explained that some "crank" had telephoned the station to report that the Mowats had painted their dog. The policemen were embarrassed, and they hastened to explain that it was the law that all such complaints had to be investigated, no matter how ridiculous they might seem. If Mother would assure them, simply for form's sake, they said, that her dog was still his natural color, they would gladly depart.

Mother at once gave them the requisite assurance, but, feeling somewhat puzzled, she hastened to the dining room to tell my father about it.

Father had vanished. He had not even finished his morning coffee. The sound of Eardlie grunting and snorting in the back alley showed that he was departing in haste.

Mother shrugged her shoulders, and began carrying the dishes out to the kitchen. At that moment Mutt scratched on the screen door. She went to let him in.

Mutt scurried into the house, with his head held low and a look of abject misery about him. He must have had a singularly bad time of it on the crowded street. He fled directly to my room, and vanished under the bed.

Father was not yet at his office when Mother phoned the library. She left an agitated message that he was to return home at once, and then she called the veterinary.

Unfortunately it was the same one who had been called in when Mutt ate the naphtha soap. He came again—but with a hard glint of suspicion in his eye.

Mother met him at the door and rushed him into the bedroom. The two of them tried to persuade Mutt to come out from under the bed. Mutt refused. Eventually the veterinary had to crawl under the bed after him—but he did this with a very poor grace.

When he emerged he was momentarily beyond speech. Mother misinterpreted his silence as a measure of the gravity of Mutt's condition. She pressed the doctor for his diagnosis. She was not prepared for the tirade he loosed upon her. He forgot all professional standards. When he left the house he was bitterly vowing that he would give up medicine and return to the wheat farm that had spawned him. He was so angry that he quite forgot the bill.

Mother had by now put up with quite enough for one morning, and she was in no condition to be further trifled with when, a few minutes later, Father came cautiously through the back door. He was almost as abject as Mutt had been. He saw the look in my mother's eye and tried to forestall her.

"I swear I didn't even guess it would do that," he explained hastily. "Surely it will wash out?" There was a pleading note in his voice.

The light of a belated understanding began to dawn on Mother. She fixed her husband with her most baleful glare.

"Will *what* wash out?" she demanded, leaving Father with no room for further evasion.

"The bluing," said my father humbly.

It was little wonder that Mother was distressed by the time I returned from my holiday. The telephone had rung almost incessantly for three days. Some of the callers were jovial—and these were undoubtedly the hardest to bear. Others were vindictive. Fortunately the reporters from the *Saskatoon Star-Phoenix* were friends of my father's and, with a notable restraint, they denied themselves the opportunity for a journalistic field day. Nevertheless, there were not many people in Saskatoon who did not know of, and who did not have opinions about, the Mowats and their bright blue dog.

By the time I arrived home Father had became very touchy

about the whole affair, and it was dangerous to question him too closely. Nevertheless, I finally dared to ask him how much bluing he had actually used.

"Just a smidgen," he replied shortly. "Just enough to take that damned yellow tint out of his fur!"

I do not know exactly how much a "smidgen" is, but I do know that when Mother asked me to clean the clogged basement drain a few days later, I removed from it a wad of paper wrappers from at least ten cubes of bluing. Some of them may, of course, have been there for some time.

4

A Flock of Ducks

IN THE FALL of the year Father and I began making preparations
for our first hunting season in the west. The weeks before the season opened were full of intense excitement and anticipation for
me, and the ordeal of school was almost unendurable. The nights
grew colder and in the hours before the dawn I would waken and
lie with a fast-beating heart listening to the majestic chanting
of the first flocks of south-bound geese. I kept my gun—a little
twenty-gauge (the first shotgun I had ever owned)—on the bed
beside me. In the sounding darkness I would lift it to my shoulder
and the room and ceiling would dissolve as the gun muzzle swung
on the track of the great voyagers.

Father was even more excited than I. Each evening he would get
out his own gun, carefully polish the glowing walnut stock, and
pack and repack the cartridges in their containers. Mother would
sit and watch him with that infuriating attitude of tolerance that
women can turn into a devastating weapon against their mates.
Mutt, on the other hand, paid no attention to our preparations
and, in fact, he grew so bored by them that he took to spending his

evenings away from home. His complete lack of interest in guns and decoys and shells and hunting clothes disgusted Father, but at the same time righteously confirmed his original estimate of Mutt.

"We'll have to hunt without a dog, Farley," he said gloomily to me one evening.

Mother, for whom this remark was actually intended, rose to the bait.

"Nonsense," she replied. "You've got Mutt—all you have to do is train him."

Father snorted derisively. "Mutt, indeed! We need a bird dog, not a bird brain."

I was stung by this reflection on Mutt's intelligence. "I think he must have bird dog in him *some*where," I said. "Look at all his 'feathers'—like a real English setter."

Father fixed me with a stern glance and beckoned me to follow him out to the garage. When we were safely in that sanctuary he shut the door.

"You've been listening to your mother again," he accused me in a tone that emphasized the gravity of this breach of masculine loyalty.

"Not really *listening*," I apologized. "She only said we ought to try him out, and maybe he might be *some* good."

Father gave me a pitying look. "You've missed the point," he explained. "Surely you're old enough by now to realize that it never pays to let a women prove she's right. It doesn't even pay to give her a chance to prove it. Mutt stays home."

My father's logic seemed confusing, but I did not argue. And so that first season we went out to the fields and sloughs without a dog. In the event, it was probably just as well. Both my father and I had a great deal to learn about hunting, and the process would have been impossibly complicated had we been attempting to train a dog at the same time.

On opening day Father and I were up long before dawn (we never really went to bed that night) and, having loaded the gun cases and all our paraphernalia into Eardlie's rumble seat, we drove through the grave desolation of the sleeping city into the open plains beyond. We drove in the making of the dawn along the straight-ruled country roads, and the dust boiled and heaved in Eardlie's wake, glowing bloody in the diffused reflection of the taillight. Occasional jack rabbits made gargantuan leaps in the cones of the headlights, or raced beside us in the ditches as ghostly outriders to the speeding little car.

The fields on either side had long since been reaped, and the grain threshed. Now the stubble was pallid and unliving, as gray as an old man's beard, in the breaking dawn. The tenuous, almost invisible lines of barbed-wire fences drew to a horizon that was unbroken except for the blunt outlines of grain elevators in unseen villages at the world's edge. Occasionally we passed a poplar bluff, already naked save for a few doomed clusters of yellowed leaves. Rarely, there was a farmhouse, slab-sided, gray, and worn by driven dust and winter gales.

I suppose it was a bleak landscape and yet it evoked in me a feeling of infinite freedom and of release that must be incomprehensible to those who dwell in the well-tamed confines of the east.

We saw no ugliness, and felt no weight of desolation. In a mood of exaltation we watched the sun leap to the horizon while the haze of fading dust clouds flared in a splendid and untrammeled flow of flame.

Many times since that morning I have seen the dawn sun on the prairie, but the hunger to see it yet again remains unsatisfied.

We turned eastward at last and drove with the sun in our eyes, and little Eardlie scattered the dust under his prancing wheels, and it was morning. My impatience could no longer be contained.

"Where do we find the birds?" I asked.

Father met my question with studied nonchalance. For almost a year he had been imbibing the lore of upland hunting. He had read many books on the subject and he had talked to a score of old-time hunters and he believed that he had already achieved expert status.

"It depends what birds you're after," he explained. "Since the chicken season isn't open yet, we're looking for Huns"—he used these colloquial names for prairie chicken and Hungarian partridge with an easy familiarity—"and Huns like to come out to the roads at dawn to gravel-up. We'll see them any time."

I mulled this over. "There isn't any gravel on these roads—only dust," I said, with what seemed to me like cogent logic.

"Of course there isn't any gravel," Father replied shortly. "Gravel-up is just an expression. In *this* case it obviously means taking a dust bath. Now keep your eyes skinned, and don't talk so much."

There was no time to pursue the matter, for a moment later Father trod hard on the brakes and Eardlie squealed a little and jolted to a halt.

A Flock of Ducks

"*There they are!*" my father whispered fiercely. "You stay near the car. I'll sneak up the ditch and flush them down the road toward you."

The light was brilliant now, but though I strained my eyes, I caught no more than a glimpse of a few grayish forms scurrying into the roadside ditch some forty yards ahead of us. Nevertheless, I loaded my gun, leaped out of the car in a fury of excitement, and crouched down by the front fender. Father had already started up the ditch, shotgun cradled in one arm, and his face almost buried in the dry vegetation. He was soon out of my sight, and for some time nothing moved upon the scene except a solitary gopher that lifted its head near a fence post and whistled derisively.

I thought that it seemed to be taking Father an interminable time, but then I did not know that he was having his first experience with Russian thistles. These are frightful weeds whose dried and thorny carcasses roll for miles across the plains each autumn, to pile up in impenetrable thickets behind the fences or in the deep roadside ditches. There had been a bumper crop of Russian thistles that year and the ditch through which Father's path lay was choked with them.

He suffered agonies, yet he persevered. Suddenly he burst out of the ditch, leveled his gun at a whirring cluster of rocketing birds, and accidentally fired both barrels at once. He disappeared again immediately, for the double recoil of a twelve-gauge shotgun is quite as formidable as a hard right to the jaw.

As Father had predicted they would, the Huns flew straight down the road toward me. I was too excited to remember to release the safety catch, but it did not matter. As the birds passed overhead I recognized them for as pretty a bevy of meadow larks as I have ever seen.

Father came back to the car after a while, and we drove on. He steered with one hand and picked thistles out of his face with the other. I did not speak, for I had a certain intuition that silence would be safer.

Nevertheless, our first day afield was not without some success. Toward evening we encountered a covey of birds and Father killed two of them with a magnificent crossing shot at thirty yards' range. We were a proud pair of hunters as we drove homeward. As we were unloading the car in front of the house, Father observed the approach of one of our neighbors and with pride held up the brace of birds to be admired.

The neighbor, a hunter of many years' experience, was impressed. He almost ran to the car and, snatching the birds out of my father's hand, he muttered:

"For God's sake, Mowat, hide those damn things quick! Don't you know the prairie-chicken season doesn't open for a week?"

Father and I learned a good deal that first autumn. We learned that the Hungarian partridge is the wiliest of birds—bullet-swift when on the wing, and approaching a gazelle in speed when running through dense cover on the ground. We became inured to the violent explosions of prairie chickens bursting out of the tall slough grass. We learned that there is only one duck that reputable western hunters deign to shoot—and that is the green-head mallard. We learned this last lesson so well that it was almost our undoing. That was on an October day when we found ten green-heads feeding placidly in a slough a few rods from an apparently abandoned farm-house. Although they seemed a little larger than the ones we had fruitlessly pursued all through the season, we never dreamed that they had an owner who was also a deputy game warden; or that any man could have such an inflated idea of the value of his livestock. At that, we escaped lightly, for the owner would undoubtedly have charged us with exceeding the bag limits—if there had been such a limit on domestic ducks.

That first season conclusively demonstrated that we really needed the services of a bird dog—if not a pointer, then at least a good retriever. We lost a number of partridge that were only winged and that ran for cover. On one occasion we came close to losing Father when he waded out into a quicksand slough to retrieve what later was identified as a double-crested cormorant. The memory of the lost birds and, in particular, of the quicksand sat heavily on Father through the following year and gave new weight to Mother's arguments as a new hunting season approached. She had a sublime faith in Mutt. Or perhaps she was just being stubborn.

My father's retreat was slow, and defended by rearguard actions. "Mutt's so obviously not a hunting dog!" he would insist as he retired a few more paces to the rear.

"Nonsense!" Mother would reply. "You know perfectly well that once Mutt makes up his mind, he can do anything. *You'll see.*"

I do not think that Father ever publicly hoisted the surrender flag. Nothing was said in so many words, but as the next hunting season drew near, it seemed to be tacitly understood that Mutt would have his chance. Mutt suspected that something unusual was afoot, but he was uncertain as to its nature. He watched curiously as Father and I salvaged our precious hunting trousers from the pile of old clothing that Mother had set aside to give to the Salvation Army (this was an annual ritual); and he sat by, looking perplexed, as we cleaned our guns and repainted the wooden duck decoys. As opening day drew closer he began to show something approaching interest in our preparations, and he even began to forgo his nightly routine check on the neighborhood garbage cans. Mother was quick to point out that this behavior indicated the awakening of some inherited sporting instinct in him. "He's started to make up his mind," Mother told us. "You wait—you'll see!"

We had not long to wait. Opening day was on a Saturday and the previous afternoon a farmer who had come to know my father through the library telephoned that immense flocks of mallards were in his stubble fields. The place was a hundred miles west of the city, so we decided to leave on Friday evening and sleep out at the farm.

We left Saskatoon at dusk. Mutt entered the car willingly enough and, having usurped the outside seat, relapsed into a dyspeptic slumber. It was too dark to see gophers, and it was too cold to press his bulbous nose into the slip stream in search of new and fascinating odors, so he slept, noisily, as Eardlie jounced over the dirt roads across the star-lit prairie. Father and I felt no need of sleep. Ahead of us we knew the great flocks were settling for the night, but we also knew that with the dawn they would

A Flock of Ducks

lift from the wide fields for the morning flight to a nearby slough where they would quench their thirst and gossip for a while, before returning to the serious business of gleaning the wheat kernels left behind by the threshing crews.

Reaching our destination at midnight, we turned from the road and drove across the fields to a haystack that stood half a mile from the slough. The penetrating warning of an early winter had come with darkness, and we had long hours to wait until the dawn. I burrowed into the side of the stack, excavating a cave for the three of us, while Father assembled the guns by the dim yellow flare of Eardlie's lights. When all was ready for the morrow Father joined me and we rolled ourselves in our blankets, there in the fragrant security of our straw cave.

I could look out through the low opening. There was a full moon—the hunter's moon—and as I watched I could see the glitter of frost crystals forming on Eardlie's hood. Somewhere far overhead—or perhaps it was only in my mind—I heard the quivering sibilance of wings. I reached out my hand and touched the cold, oily barrel of my gun lying in the straw beside me; and I knew a quality of happiness that has not been mine since that long-past hour.

Mutt did not share my happiness. He was never fond of sleeping out, and on this chill night there was no pleasure for him in the frosty fields or in that shining sky. He was suspicious of the dubious comforts of our cave, suspecting perhaps that it was some kind of trap, and he had refused to budge from the warm seat of the car.

The Dog Who Wouldn't Be

An hour or so after I had dozed off I was abruptly awakened when, from somewhere near at hand, a coyote lifted his penetrating quaver into the chill air. Before the coyote's song had reached the halfway mark, Mutt shot into the cave, ricocheted over Father, and came to a quivering halt upon my stomach. I grunted under the impact, and angrily heaved him off. There followed a good deal of confused shoving and pushing in the darkness, while Father muttered scathing words about "hunting dogs" that were frightened of a coyote's wail. Mutt did not reply, but, having pulled down a large portion of the straw roof upon our heads, curled up across my chest and feigned sleep.

I was awakened again before dawn by a trickle of straw being dislodged upon me by exploring mice, and by the chatter of juncos in the stubble outside the cave. I nudged my father and sleepily we began the battle with greasy boots and moisture-laden clothing. Mutt was in the way. He steadfastly refused to rise at such an ungodly hour, and in the end had to be dragged out of the warm shelter. Whatever hunting instincts he had inherited seemed to have atrophied overnight. We were not sanguine about his potential value to us as we cooked our breakfast over the hissing blue flame of a little gasoline stove.

When at length we finished our coffee and set off across the frost-brittle stubble toward the slough, Mutt grudgingly agreed to accompany us only because he did not wish to be left behind with the coyotes.

It was still dark, but there was a faint suggestion of a gray luminosity in the east as we felt our way through the bordering poplar bluffs to the slough and to a reed duck-blind that the farmer had built for us. The silence seemed absolute and the cold had a rare intensity that knifed through my clothes and left me shivering at its touch. Wedged firmly between my knees, as we squatted behind the blind, Mutt also shivered, muttering gloomily the while about the foolishness of men and boys who would deliberately expose themselves and their dependents to such chill discomfort.

I paid little heed to his complaints, for I was watching for the dawn. Shaken by excitement as much as by the cold, I waited with straining eyes and ears while an aeon passed. Then, with the abruptness of summer lightning, the dawn was on us. Through the blurred screen of leafless trees I beheld the living silver of the slough, miraculously conjured out of the dark mists. The shimmering surface was rippled by the slow, waking movements of two green-winged teal, and at the sight of them my heart thudded with a wild beat. My gloved hand tightened on Mutt's collar until he squirmed, and I glanced down at him and saw, to my surprise, that his attitude of sullen discontent had been replaced by one of acute, if somewhat puzzled, interest. Perhaps something of what I myself was feeling had been communicated to him, or perhaps Mother had been right about his inheritance. I had no time to think upon it, for the flight was coming in.

We heard it first—a low and distant vibration that was felt as much as heard, but that soon grew to a crescendo of deep-pitched sound, as if innumerable artillery shells were rushing upon us through the resisting air. I heard Father's wordless exclamation and, peering over the lip of the blind, I saw the yellow sky go dark as a living cloud obscured it. And then the massed wings enveloped us and the sound was the roar of a great ocean beating into the caves of the sea.

As I turned my face up in wonderment to that incredible vision, I heard Father whisper urgently, "They'll circle once at least. Hold your fire till they start pitching in."

Now the whole sky was throbbing with their wings. Five—ten thousand of them perhaps, they banked away and the roar receded, swelled and renewed itself, and the moment was almost at hand. I let go of Mutt's collar in order to release the safety catch on my shotgun.

Mutt went insane.

That, anyway, is the most lenient explanation I can give for what he did. From a sitting start he leaped straight up into the air high enough to go clear over the front of the blind, and when he hit the ground again he was running at a speed that he had never before attained, and never would again. And he was vocal. Screaming and yelping with hysterical abandon, he looked, and sounded, like a score of dogs.

Father and I fired at the now rapidly receding flocks, but that was no more than a gesture—a release for our raging spirits. Then we dropped the useless guns and hurled terrible words after our bird dog.

We might as well have saved our breath. I do not think he even heard us. Straight over the shining fields he flew, seemingly almost air-borne himself, while the high flight of frightened ducks cast its shadow over him. He became a steadily diminishing dot in an illimitable distance, and then he vanished and the world grew silent.

The words we might have used, one to the other, as we sat down against the duck blind, would all have been inadequate. We said nothing. We simply waited. The sun rose high and red and the light grew until it was certain that there would be no more ducks that morning, and then we went back to the car and brewed some coffee. And then we waited.

He came back two hours later. He came so circumspectly (hugging the angles of the fences) that I did not see him until he was fifty yards away from the car. He was a sad spectacle. Dejection showed in every line from the dragging tail to the abject flop of his ears. He had evidently failed to catch a duck.

For Father that first experience with Mutt was bitter-sweet. True enough we had lost the ducks—but as a result my father was in a fair way to regain the initiative against Mother on the home front. This first skirmish had gone his way. But he was not one to rest on victory. Consequently, during the first week of the season we shot no birds at all, while Mutt demonstrated with what seemed to be an absolute certainty that he was not, and never would be, a bird dog.

It is true that Mutt, still smarting from the failure of his first effort, tried hard to please us, yet it seemed to be impossible for him to grasp the real point of our excursions into the autumnal plains.

On the second day out he decided that we must be after gophers and he spent most of that day digging energetically into their deep burrows. He got nothing for his trouble save an attack of asthma from too much dust in his nasal passages.

The third time out he concluded that we were hunting cows.

That was a day that will live long in memory. Mutt threw himself into cow chasing with a frenzy that was almost fanatical. He became, in a matter of hours, a dedicated dog. It was a ghastly day, yet it had its compensations for Father. When we returned home that night, very tired, very dusty—and sans birds—he was able to report gloatingly to Mother that her "hunting dog" had attempted to retrieve forty-three heifers, two bulls, seventy-two steers, and an aged ox belonging to a Dukhobor family.

It must have seemed to my father that his early judgment of Mutt was now unassailable. But he should have been warned by the tranquility with which Mother received his account of the day's events.

Mother's leap from the quaking bog to rock-firm ground was so spectacular that it left me breathless; and it left Father so stunned that he could not even find reply.

Mother smiled complacently at him.

"Poor, dear Mutt," she said. "*He* knows the dreadful price of beef these days."

5

Mallard-Pool-Mutt

I HAD supposed that after the fiascos of that first week of hunting, Mutt would be banned from all further expeditions. It seemed a logical supposition, even though logic was often the stranger in our home. Consequently I was thoroughly startled one morning to find the relative positions of the antagonists in our family's battle of the sexes reversed. At breakfast Mother elaborated on her new theme that Mutt was far too sensible to waste his time hunting game birds; and Father replied with the surprising statement that he could train any dog to do anything, and that Mutt could, and would, become the "best damn bird dog in the west!" I thought that my father was being more than usually rash, but he thought otherwise, and so throughout the rest of that season Mutt accompanied us on every shooting trip, and he and Father struggled with one another in a conflict that at times reached epic proportions.

The trouble was that Mutt, having discovered the joys of cattle running, infinitely preferred cows to birds. The task of weaning him away from cattle chasing to an interest in game birds seemed hopeless. Yet Father persevered with such determination that toward the end of the season he began to see some meager prospect of success. On those rare occasions when Mutt allowed us to shoot a bird we would force the corpse into his jaws, or hang it, albatrosslike, about his neck, for him to bring back to the car. He deeply resented this business, for the feathers of upland game birds made him sneeze, and the oily taste of duck feathers evidently gave him a mild form of nausea. Eventually, however, he was persuaded to pick up a dead Hungarian partridge of his own volition, but he did this only because Father had made it clear to him that there would be no more cow chasing that day if he refused to humor us. Finally, on a day in early October, he stumbled on a dead partridge, without having it pointed out to him, and, probably because there were no cows in sight and he was bored, he picked it up and brought it back. That first real retrieve was not an unqualified success, since Mutt did not have what dog fanciers refer to as a "tender mouth." When we received the partridge we got no more than a bloody handful of feathers. We did not dare complain.

Being determinedly optimistic, we took this incident as a hopeful sign, and redoubled our efforts. But Mutt remained primarily a cow chaser; and it was not until the final week end of the hunting season that the tide began to turn.

As the result of a book-distributing plan which he had organized, my father had become acquainted with an odd assortment of people scattered all through the province. One of these was a Ukrainian immigrant named Paul Sazalisky. Paul owned two

Mallard-Pool-Mutt

sections on the shores of an immense slough known as Middle Lake that lies well to the east of Saskatoon. On Thursday of the last week of the season, Paul phoned Father to report that huge flocks of Canada geese were massing on the lake. He invited us to come out and try our luck.

That was a frigid journey. Snow already lay upon the ground and the north wind was so bitter that Mutt did not leap out after cattle even once. He stayed huddled up on the floor boards over the manifold heater, inhaling gusts of hot air and carbon monoxide.

We arrived at Middle Lake in the early evening and found a wasteland that even to our eyes seemed the essence of desolation. Not a tree pierced the gray emptiness. The roads had subsided into freezing gumbo tracks and they seemed to meander without hope across a lunar landscape. The search for Paul's farm was long and agonizing.

Paul's house, when at last we found it, turned out to be a clay-plastered shanty perched like a wart upon the face of the whitened plains. It was unprepossessing in appearance. There were only two rooms, each with a single tiny window—yet it held Paul, his wife, his wife's parents, Paul's seven children, and two cousins who had been recruited to help with the pigs. The pigs, as we soon discovered, were the mainstay of the establishment, and their aroma was everywhere. It seemed to me to be a singularly unpleasant odor too—far worse than that usually associated with pigs. But there was a good reason for the peculiarly powerful properties of that memorable stench.

Like most of the immigrants who came from middle Europe

in response to the lure of free land in Canada, Paul was an astute and farsighted fellow. As soon as he had taken over his homestead on the shores of Middle Lake, he made a thorough assessment of the natural resources at his disposal. He soon discovered that a narrow channel which flowed through his property, connecting the two main arms of Middle Lake, was crowded with enormous suckers. There was no commercial market for these soft-fleshed fish, so they had remained undisturbed until Paul came, and saw, and was inspired. Paul concluded that if the fish could not be marketed in their present form, their flesh might very well be sold if it was converted into a more acceptable product—such as pork.

He surprised his wheat-farming neighbors by going into the pig business on a large scale.

He acquired three dip nets, and began to raise hogs on suckers. The hogs prospered almost unbelievably on this pure protein diet, reaching marketable weight in about two thirds the length of time required by corn-fed swine. They bred with abandon, and their progeny were insatiable for fish.

Paul was a bit of a mystery man locally. None of his neighbors knew about the fish, and there were two good reasons for Paul's reticence. First of all, he had no wish to share a good thing with duller folk; and secondly, he had sometimes tasted fish-fed swine in the Ukraine. Because of this experience he chose to ship his hogs all the way to Winnipeg, disdaining the more accessible local markets, and cheerfully shouldering the extra freight costs. The local people thought that this was foolish, but Paul saw no reason to explain that he had chosen Winnipeg because it would be practically impossible for the retail butchers in that large city to trace the origin of certain hams and sides of bacon which seemed to have been cured in cod-liver oil.

In later years Paul became a powerful and respected figure in the west. He was of the stuff from which great men are made.

He was still in the preliminary stages of his career when we knew him and he had few physical amenities to offer guests. Nevertheless, when Eardlie drew up at his door, he took us to the bosom of his family.

That is to say he took Father and me to the family bosom. Mutt refused to be taken. Sniffing the heavy air about the cabin with ill-concealed disgust, he at first refused even to leave the car. He sat on the seat, his nose dripping, saying "Faugh!" at frequent intervals. It was not until full darkness had brought with it the breath of winter, and the wailing of the coyotes, that he came scratching at the cabin door.

We three slept on the floor, as did most of Paul's family, for there was only one bed in the place. The floor had its advantages since the air at the lower levels contained some oxygen. There was none too much and, since neither of the two windows could be opened, the trickle of fresh air that found its way under the door was soon lost in a swirl of nameless other gases. Our lungs worked overtime, and we sweated profusely, for the stove remained volcanic the night through.

For Father and me it was a difficult experience. For Mutt it was sheer hell. Gasping for breath, he squirmed about the floor, seeking relief and finding none. Finally he thrust his nose under my armpit and resigned himself to what seemed like certain suffocation.

For once in his life Mutt was delighted to rise before the sun. When Mrs. Sazalisky opened the door at 4 A.M. to get some poplar billets with which to cook our breakfast, Mutt staggered from the room moaning audibly. He had not yet fully recovered an hour later when Paul guided us down to the soggy shores of the lake and out along a low mud spit.

At the tip of the spit Paul had previously dug two foxholes for us. There was water in the holes, and it was ice-encrusted. The mud was stiff and frigid. There was a nasty wind out of the northwest and, although it was still too dark to see, we could feel the sharp bite of driven snow in our faces.

Paul left us after a murmured injunction to keep an eye out for flocks coming from behind, and we three settled down to wait the dawn.

In retrospect I cannot recall ever having been so cold. Not even the excitement of waiting for my first shot at a goose could keep the blood flowing to my numb extremities. As for Mutt, he was soon beyond all feeling. We had found a sack for him to lie on, but it did him little good. He began to shiver extravagantly, and then to snuffle, and finally his teeth began to chatter. Father and I were surprised by this, for neither of us had ever heard a dog's teeth chatter before. We had not thought that such a thing was possible. Nevertheless, all through that interminable wait Mutt's teeth rang like a cascade of gravel. He was so cold that he no longer even complained, and we recognized this as a bad sign, for when Mutt could not complain he was near the last extremity.

The dawn, when it came at last, was gray and somber. The sky lightened so imperceptibly that we could hardly detect the coming of the morning. Father and I strained our eyes over the wind-driven water and then, suddenly, we heard the sound of wings. Cold was forgotten. We crouched in the flooded holes and flexed our numb fingers in their shooting gloves.

Father saw them first. He nudged me sharply and I half turned my head to behold a spectacle of incomparable grandeur. Out of the gray storm scud, like ghostly ships, a hundred whistling swans drove down upon us on their heavy wings. They passed directly overhead, not half a gunshot from us, and we were lost beyond time and space in a moment of unparalleled majesty and mystery. Then they were gone, and the snow eddies once again obscured our straining vision.

It would not have mattered greatly after that if we had seen no other living thing all day, nor fired a single shot. But the swans were only the leaders of a multitude. The windy silence of the mud spit was soon pierced by the sonorous cries of seemingly endless flocks of geese that drifted wraithlike overhead. They were flying low that day, so we could see them clearly. Snow geese, startlingly white of breast, with jet-black wing tips, beat past the point, and small bands of waveys kept formation with them like outriders. The honkers came close behind, and as the rush of air through their great pinions sounded harsh above the wind, Father and I stood up and raised our guns. A flight came low directly over us, and we fired as one. The sound of the shots seemed puny, and was lost at once in that immensity of wind and water.

It was pure mischance that one of the birds was hit, for, as we admitted to each other later, neither of us had really aimed at those magnificent gray presences. Nevertheless, one of them fell, appearing gigantic and primeval in the tenuous light as it spiraled sharply down. It struck the water a hundred yards from shore and we saw with dismay that it had only been winged, for it swam off at once, with neck outthrust, after the vanishing flock.

We ran to the shore, and we were frantic. It was not entirely the prospect of losing the goose that distracted us; rather it was the knowledge that we could not leave that great bird to perish slowly amidst the gathering ice. We had no boat. Paul had promised to return after dawn with a little dugout; but there was no sign of him, and the goose was now swimming strongly toward the outer limit of our vision.

We had quite forgotten Mutt. We were astounded when he suddenly appeared beside us, cast one brief glance at the disappearing bird, and leaped into the bitter waters.

To this day I have no idea what prompted him. Perhaps it was because the goose, being very large, seemed more worthy of his efforts than any duck had ever been. Perhaps he was simply so cold and miserable that the death wish was on him. But I do not really believe either of these explanations. I think my mother was right, and that from somewhere in his inscrutable ancestry a memory had at long last come to life.

The snow flurries had grown heavier and Mutt and the goose

soon vanished from our view. We waited through interminable minutes, and when he did not reappear we began to be frightened for him. We called, but if he heard us down the wind, he did not respond. At length Father ran off down the mud spit to seek Paul and the boat, leaving me alone with a growing certainty that I had seen my dog for the last time.

The relief was almost overwhelming when, some minutes later, I caught a glimpse of Mutt returning out of the lowering scud. He was swimming hard, but the wind and seas were against him and it was some time before I could see him clearly. He had the goose firmly by one wing, but the honker was fighting fiercely. It seemed inconceivable that Mutt could succeed in bringing it to shore and I was convinced that he would drown before my very eyes. Many times he was driven completely under water, yet each time, when he emerged, his grip upon the goose remained unbroken. The goose buffeted him across the face with its uninjured wing; it jumped on his head; it attempted to fly; it attempted to dive; yet Mutt held on.

When he was still twenty feet from shore I could bear the strain no longer and I waded out into the shallows until I was hip-deep. Mutt saw me and turned my way. When he came within reach I grabbed the goose from him and promptly discovered that it was as formidable as it appeared to be. It was all I could do to haul it ashore, and I suffered a buffeting in the process that left my legs and arms bruised for many a day.

Paul and Father arrived in the little boat a short time later. They hurried ashore and Paul stood looking down at Mutt, who was now swathed in my hunting coat. I was sitting on the goose, and barely managing to keep it under control.

"By God!" Paul said, and there was awe in his voice. "By God! You shoot the *big* gray goose! And dat dam' dog—he bring him back? By God! I don't believe!"

Mutt wriggled under the coat and one eye opened. Life was returning; for if there was one thing that could stir him from the edge of the grave itself, it was honest praise. He must have recognized Paul's incredulity as the highest praise indeed.

We carried him back to the cabin and when Mrs. Sazalisky heard the story, she gave him a hero's welcome. He was placed beside the red-hot stove and fed enormous quantities of steaming goulash. Only when he had begun to burp uncontrollably from the combination of too much heat and too much food, did his hostess desist from filling up his plate.

We all made much of him, both then and later when we returned home. Never before had Mutt received such adulation, and he found it good. We could not anticipate it at the time, but when the hunting season rolled around a year later, we were to discover that cows, gophers, and even cats (during the shooting season at least) had been erased forever from his list of loves.

Once Mutt had made up his mind to be a bird dog, there was no further question of his being "trained." Nothing could have been more superfluous than the attempt. If any training was done at all, then it was Father and I who were the trainees. For Mutt soon displayed an incredible array of hidden talents. And if he was completely unorthodox, he was indisputably brilliant in his new career.

Mallard-Pool-Mutt

The nature of this new Mutt became apparent on opening day of the duck season in the following year.

By coincidence we had returned once more to the slough where Mutt had disgraced himself on his first hunting expedition. That slough, still nameless then, is now renowned to sportsmen throughout the west as Mallard-Pool-Mutt, and this is the tale of how it got its name.

We did not sleep out on this occasion, but drove direct from home, arriving just in time to hurry into the blind before day broke. We had Mutt on a leash, for his exploit at Middle Lake had not completely erased our memory of the debacle which had resulted from his first visit to the slough. We had hopes that he would redeem himself this time—but we were cautious. We even considered the advisability of muzzling him so that he would not scream the ducks away again; but this ignominy would have been too much for him to bear, and so we risked his voice.

It was a different dawn, and yet the same as that which we had seen two years before. Once more the red glare of the morning sun fell on the immaculate mirror of the pond; and once more there was a pair of ducks—pintails this time—sleepily dabbling among the long reeds by the shore. The same pungent odor of salt and muck—an odor that is tasted rather than smelled—rose to us on the edgings of gray mist along the borders of the slough. And the same taut expectation lay upon us as we waited for the morning flight.

The flight, too, came as it had done before, and as it had probably done since this slough was born. Out of the northern sky, half lit now, the sound of its approach was like a rush of wind.

The Dog Who Wouldn't Be

We crouched lower in the blind and my grip tightened warningly on Mutt's collar. Once more I felt him tremble under my hand, and I was vaguely aware that he was making odd little whimpering cries deep in his throat. But my attention was on the approaching flocks.

They came in with a great "whoosh" as the leaders thrust out their feet and struck and shattered the calm surface of the pool. They came in such numbers that it seemed the slough would be too small to hold them all—and still they came.

There was no premature fusillade this time. Father and I were no longer tyros—and Mutt was securely tethered. We stood up together and the crash of the guns echoed like the hint of distant thunder amidst a swirling hurricane of stiff and frantic wings. It was all over in less than a minute. The sky was clear above us and the silence had returned. Out on the slough eight ducks remained, and five of them were greenhead drakes.

Mutt was almost tearing the leash from my hands as we left the blind. "Let him go," my father said. "He can't do any harm now. Let's see what he makes of this."

I slipped the leash. Mutt went through the band of muck and sedge at the water's edge like a kangaroo, in great ungainly leaps. The last jump took him well into deep water, and he began churning forward like an old-fashioned stern-wheeler. There was a wild, almost mad glint in his eyes and he had the look of impetuous resolution about him that belongs naturally to a charging buffalo.

Father and I stared at each other, and then at Mutt, in dumb amaze. But when we saw him reach the first dead duck, snap his teeth fast in a wing tip, and start for shore with it, we knew that we had found us a retrieving dog.

What Mutt had done up to this point was, of course, no more than any good bird dog would have done. But the events that followed unmistakably presaged the flowering of his unique genius.

The signs were blurred at first, for though he brought the first dead duck to shore all right, he made no attempt to deliver it properly into our hands. He simply dropped it on the verge and turned at once to make the next retrieve.

However, as long as he brought the ducks to land, we saw no reason to complain—at least we saw no reason until he had retrieved the three dead ducks and had begun work on the remaining five, all of which were still quite active.

Then he began to have difficulties. It took him several minutes to swim-down the first cripple, but eventually he managed to catch it by a wing tip and drag it to the shore. He deposited it unceremoniously, and at once leaped back into the water. Hard on his heels, the duck followed suit. Mutt did not notice, for his attention was already fixed on another duck in mid-pond.

It was a large slough, and very soft and treacherous near the edge. Try as we might, neither Father nor I could manage to be on hand when Mutt brought the cripples in. Neither could we put the wounded birds out of their pain, as we should have liked to do, since we were not able to get within gunshot of them. It was all up to Mutt.

By the time he had retrieved fifteen out of the original eight ducks, he was beginning to grow annoyed. His first fresh enthusiasm was wearing thin, but his brain was beginning to function. The next duck he brought ashore followed the routine already established by it and its fellows and, as soon as Mutt's back was turned, waddled into the pond. This time Mutt kept a wary eye cocked over his shoulder, and he saw that he was being had.

Father and I were at the far end of the pond, and we watched to see how he would react now that he knew the worst. Treading water in mid-pond, he turned and stared at us with a look of mingled scorn and disgust, as if to say: "What on earth's the matter with you? You've got legs, haven't you? Expect me to do *all* the work?"

The situation suddenly struck us as being vastly amusing, and we began to laugh. Mutt never could stand being laughed at, though he enjoyed being laughed with; and he turned his back and began to swim to the far end of the pond. We thought for a moment he had abandoned the ducks and was about to take himself off. We were wrong.

With not so much as another glance in our direction, he swam to the far side of the slough, turned about, and painstakingly began to herd all the crippled ducks toward our end of the pond.

When all of them, save one old greenhead which skillfully evaded the roundup by diving, were within easy shotgun range of our position, Mutt turned and swam nonchalantly away again.

We did our duty, but with a strong feeling of unreality upon us. "Do you think he did that on purpose?" Father asked me in awe-struck tones.

Mallard-Pool-Mutt

Mutt had now gone back for the remaining mallard. This one was a magnificent drake, perhaps the leader of the flight, and he was cunning with his years. His injury must have been slight, for it was all Mutt could do to close the gap between them. And then, when Mutt was near enough to lunge, his teeth snapped shut on nothing but a mouthful of water. The drake had dived again.

We watched as, three times, the drake evaded capture in this manner, leaving Mutt to swim in aimless circles on the surface.

The old bird chose his water, and stayed well away from shore, for he knew about guns. We concluded finally that this was one duck we would not get, and we decided to call Mutt in.

He was growing very weary. As his coat became increasingly water-logged he swam lower and lower, and his speed diminished to the point where he could just manage to overhaul the drake, and that was all. Nevertheless, he ignored us when we called to him, gently at first, and then in commanding tones. We began to be afraid that, in this willful obstinacy, he would drown himself. Father had already begun to strip off his hunting jacket and boots, ready to effect a rescue, when the incredible thing happened.

Mutt had closed with his quarry for the fifth time. The duck waited, and at the last instant again upended and disappeared.

This time Mutt also disappeared.

A swirl of muddy water marked his passing, and in the center of the swirl there was a whitish blob that twisted back and forth lethargically. I recognized it as the tip of Mutt's tail, held aloft by the remaining buoyancy in his long feathers.

Father was already wading through the muck when my startled

yell halted him. Together we stood and stared, and could not credit the reality of what we saw.

Mutt had reappeared. Weed festooned his face, and his eyes were bulging horribly. He gasped for breath and floundered heavily. But between his front teeth was the tip of the drake's wing.

When at last Mutt lay before us, panting and half drowned, we were a humbled and penitent man and boy. I rolled the leash up in my hand and, catching Father's glance, I turned and threw it with all my strength far out into the slough.

It sank with hardly a ripple into the still depths of Mallard-Pool-Mutt.

6

Mutt Makes His Mark

ONCE Mutt had fully dedicated himself as a retriever, our hunting expeditions became pure joy, unadulterated by the confusion and chaos which were so much a part of our life in the city. I looked forward hungrily to the days when the brazen harvest would be made, and the fields lie cropped and crisp beneath our boots, the days when the poplar leaves would spin to earth, and the frost would harden the saline muck about the little sloughs, the days when dawn would come like a crystalline shock out of a sky that held no clouds, save those vital ones that were the flocks pursuing their long way south.

Yet if I looked forward with a consuming eagerness to those days, then Mutt's anticipation far surpassed mine. Having found a purpose in his life, he became so avid for the hunt that in the final weeks before the season opened he would become impervious to all ordinary temptations. Cats could wander at will across his own lawn, not a dozen feet from his twitching nose, and he would not even see them. The honeyed breeze from the house next door, where a lovely little cocker bitch yearned in lonely isolation, had no power to wake him from his dreams. He lay on the browning lawn beside the garage and did not take his eyes from the doors through which Eardlie would soon emerge to carry him, and us, into the living plains.

Each season he went absolutely mad on the first day, and each season when he retrieved his first bird, he brought back a badly mangled corpse. But that never happened twice in a given year. And after that first outburst he would steady to his job.

There seemed to be no limits to his capacity for self-improvement as a hunting dog. Each season he devised new refinements designed to bring him nearer to perfection; and some of these were more than passing strange.

One Wednesday in early October we introduced a friend from Ontario to prairie hunting. He owned a whole kennel of purebred setters, and he had hunted upland birds in the east for thirty years. He was a man who could seldom be surprised by the sagacity of dogs. Yet Mutt surprised and even startled him.

Although he was clearly taken aback by Mutt's appearance, our friend refrained from casting any doubts upon the glowing character which we gave our dog, and as a result of this act of faith he and Mutt got on well from the outset of their acquaintance. On the Wednesday of which I write, the two of them went off together around one side of a large poplar bluff, while Father and I went around the other side. Our mutual objective was a covey of Hungarian partridges which we knew to be lurking somewhere near at hand.

Now Hungarian partridges have survived and multiplied even

where the hunting pressure is severest and there is good reason why this is so. Once the fusillade of opening day has alerted them, they become, for the most part, quite untouchable. Crouched invisible in the stubble, they see you long before you see them, and when you have closed to within forty or fifty yards, they burst upward like so many land mines; the flock disperses in as many directions as there are birds, and at bulletlike speed. They hit the ground running, and never stop running until they are miles away. And they seem to run just a little faster than they fly.

Our eastern friend knew all of this, in theory anyway. He was properly alert when the flock flushed at fifty yards to vanish almost immediately into a willow swale. Nevertheless, he did not even have time to pull a trigger. He was chagrined by this failure. And then to make matters worse Mutt suddenly disobeyed the cardinal bird-dog law, and without so much as an apologetic look at his companion, he raced after the vanished flock.

Our friend whistled, called him, swore at him, but to no avail. Mutt galloped away in his quaint and lopsided fashion and soon was out of sight.

We rejoined our guest at the far side of the poplar bluff, and though he had the grace to say nothing, it was easy enough to guess his thoughts. But it was not so easy to guess them when, a few minutes later, there was a great huffing and puffing from behind us and we turned to see Mutt approaching at a trot, and bearing a partridge in his mouth.

Our friend was frankly overcome.

"What the devil!" he cried. "I never fired my gun. Don't tell me this paragon of yours doesn't even need a gunner's help?"

Father laughed in a condescending sort of way.

"Oh, not quite that," he explained with his usual flair for the dramatic. "Mutt gets more birds, of course, if he has a gun to help him—but he does pretty well without. He runs them down, you know."

Father did not bother to complete the explanation, and our friend returned to the distant east somewhat dissatisfied with his fine kennel stock, and only after a determined but useless attempt to take Mutt with him. He was a man who believed his eyes, and he did not know, as we did, that the unshot Hungarian had been a running cripple, probably wounded by another hunter sometime earlier.

Nevertheless, Mutt's abilities in this regard were not to be treated lightly. He often spotted a cripple in a flock when we could not, and on at least a dozen different occasions he made a retrieve when we, who had not fired, were morally certain there was nothing to retrieve. We learned not to waste adrenaline cursing at him when he abandoned normal procedure and went off on his own. It was too embarrassing, apologizing to him when he returned later with a bird in his mouth.

There was no place where a wounded bird was safe from him. His strangely bulbous nose, uncouth as it appeared, was singularly efficient in the field and he could find birds that were apparently unfindable.

There were numbers of ruffed grouse in the poplar bluffs to the north of Saskatoon and occasionally we hunted these wily birds. They clung close to cover and were hard to hit. But once hit, they were always ours, for Mutt could find them though they hid in the most unlikely places.

One frosty morning near Wakaw Lake I slightly wounded a grouse and watched with disappointment as it flew across a wide intervening morass, and disappeared into the maze of upper branches of a diamond-willow clump. Mutt galloped off at once, but I was certain he would find no trace of it. Without hope I set out to follow him across the muskeg, and I was only nicely started on my way when I saw a considerable disturbance in the diamond-willow clump. The heavy growth—some twenty feet in height—began to sway and crackle. I stopped and stared, and in due time I saw a flash of white, and then beheld Mutt's head above the crown of the tree, with the ruffed grouse in his mouth—as usual.

He had some difficulty getting back to the ground, and he was rather disheveled when he finally reached me. But he accepted my congratulations calmly. He took such things as this high-level retrieve quite for granted.

Even the open sky offered no sure sanctuary from him, for I have seen him leap six or eight feet in the air to haul down a slow-starting and slightly wounded prairie chicken or Hungarian. As for the water—the wounded duck that thought water offered safety was mortally in ignorance.

Mutt never became resigned to the oily taste of ducks, and he always brought them in by holding the tip of their wing feathers between his front teeth—with his lips curled back, as if the duck stank of some abominable odor. As a result of his distaste for them he could never bring himself to kill a duck, and this reluctance sometimes caused him trouble.

There was a time at Meota Lake when my father and I had been lucky enough to knock down five mallards with four shots. Unfortunately, the birds were all alive, and actively so, although they could not fly. Mutt went after them, but it was a very swampy shore, and it was all he could do to wade through the marsh unimpeded. It was almost impossible for him to return to firm ground with a flapping mallard in his mouth. He solved the problem by carrying his retrieves to a tiny islet in the lake, while we went off to find a boat.

When we reached the islet, a half hour later, we found a fantastic situation. There was Mutt, and there were the five ducks, but all of them were on the move. One, two, or three at a time, the ducks would waddle off toward the water, and Mutt would dash between them and freedom and herd them back to the high ground. Then he would snatch at the wing of one, sit—literally—on another, hold two down with his paws, and try to maneuver his belly over the fifth. But the fifth would manage to get free, and scuttle away. Whereupon Mutt would have to abandon all his prisoners; they would all dash off, and he would have it all to do over again. He was about at the end of his tether when we came to his rescue, and it was the only time on a hunting trip that I ever saw him really harassed. How he managed to get those five struggling birds to the island in the first place I do not know.

Mutt Makes His Mark

He had long since perfected his diving technique, and could attain depths of five feet and stay under for as long as a minute. He soon learned, too, that in the case of a deep-diving duck it was sometimes possible to tire it out by waiting on the surface at the point where it would most probably rise, and then forcing it under again before it had time to breathe.

Only once did I see him beaten by a duck—and that time it was no real duck, but a western grebe. Mutt had already retrieved a bufflehead for us, and had gone back out in the belief that a second bird awaited his attention. We could not persuade him otherwise. Knowing how useless it was to argue with him, we let him have his way, although the grebe was quite uninjured—at least by any shot of ours.

Grebes seldom fly, but they dive like fish, and Mutt spent the best part of an hour chasing that bird while Father and I concealed ourselves in the duck blind, and tried to muffle our mirth. It would never have done to let Mutt know we were amused. He did not appreciate humor when he was its butt.

He got more and more exasperated and, though the water was ten or fifteen feet deep, he finally gave up trying to tire the grebe and decided to go down after it. But he was not built for really deep diving. His buoyancy was too great, and he was badly ballasted. At the third attempt he turned-turtle under the water and popped to the surface upside down. Then and only then did he reluctantly come ashore. We set off at once to hunt grouse so that he could get the taste of defeat out of his mouth, and otherwise relieve himself of about a gallon of lake water.

The Dog Who Wouldn't Be

Word of Mutt's phenomenal abilities soon got around, for neither my father nor I was reticent about him. At first the local hunters were skeptical, but after some of them had seen him work, their disbelief began to change into a strong civic pride that, in due time, made Mutt's name a byword for excellence in Saskatchewan hunting circles.

Indeed, Mutt became something of a symbol—a truly western symbol, for his feats were sometimes slightly exaggerated by his partisans for the benefit of unwary strangers—particularly if the strangers came out of the east. It was an encounter between just such a stranger and some of Mutt's native admirers that brought him to his greatest and most lasting triumph—a success that will not be forgotten in Saskatoon while there are birds, and dogs to hunt them.

It all began on one of those blistering July days when the prairie pants like a dying coyote, the dust lies heavy, and the air burns the flesh it touches. On such days those with good sense retire to the cellar caverns that are euphemistically known in Canada as beer parlors. These are all much the same across the country—ill-lit and crowded dens, redolent with the stench of sweat, spilled beer, and smoke—but they are, for the most part, moderately cool. And the insipid stuff that passes for beer is usually ice cold.

On this particular day five residents of the city, dog fanciers all, had forgathered in a beer parlor. They had just returned from witnessing some hunting-dog trials held in Manitoba, and they had brought a guest with them. He was a rather portly gentleman from the state of New York, and he had both wealth and ambition.

Mutt Makes His Mark

He used his wealth lavishly to further his ambition, which was to raise and own the finest retrievers on the continent, if not in the world. Having watched his own dogs win the Manitoba trials, this man had come on to Saskatoon at the earnest invitation of the local men, in order to see what kind of dogs they bred, and to buy some if he fancied them.

He had not fancied them. Perhaps rightfully annoyed at having made the trip in the broiling summer weather to no good purpose, he had become a little overbearing in his manner. His comments when he viewed the local kennel dogs had been acidulous, and scornful. He had ruffled the local breeders' feelings, and as a result they were in a mood to do and say foolish things.

The visitor's train was due to leave at 4 P.M., and from 12:30 until 3 the six men sat cooling themselves internally, and talking dogs. The talk was as heated as the weather. Inevitably Mutt's name was mentioned, and he was referred to as an outstanding example of that rare breed, the Prince Albert retriever.

The stranger hooted. "Rare breed!" he cried. "I'll say it must be rare! I've never even heard of it."

The local men were incensed by this big-city skepticism. They immediately began telling tales of Mutt, and if they laid it on a little, who can blame them? But the more stories they told, the louder grew the visitor's mirth and the more pointed his disbelief. Finally someone was goaded a little too far.

"I'll bet you," Mutt's admirer said truculently, "I'll bet you a hundred dollars this dog can outretrieve any damn dog in the whole United States."

[79]

Perhaps he felt that he was safe, since the hunting season was not yet open. Perhaps he was too angry to think.

The stranger accepted the challenge, but it did not seem as if there was much chance of settling the bet. Someone said as much, and the visitor crowed.

"You've made your brag," he said. "Now show me."

There was nothing for it then but to seek out Mutt and hope for inspiration. The six men left the dark room and braved the blasting light of the summer afternoon as they made their way to the public library.

The library stood, four-square and ugly, just off the main thoroughfare of the city. The inevitable alley behind it was shared by two Chinese restaurants and by sundry other merchants. My father had his office in the rear of the library building overlooking the alley. A screened door gave access to whatever air was to be found trapped and roasted in the narrow space behind the building. It was through this rear door that the delegation came.

From his place under the desk Mutt barely raised his head to peer at the newcomers, then sank back into a comatose state of near oblivion engendered by the heat. He probably heard the mutter of talk, the introductions, and the slightly strident tone of voice of the stranger, but he paid no heed.

Father, however, listened intently. And he could hardly control his resentment when the stranger stooped, peered beneath the desk, and was heard to say, "*Now* I recognize the breed—Prince Albert rat hound did you say it was?"

Mutt Makes His Mark

My father got stiffly to his feet. "You gentlemen wish a demonstration of Mutt's retrieving skill—is that it?" he asked.

A murmur of agreement from the local men was punctuated by a derisive comment from the visitor. "Test him," he said offensively. "How about that alley there—it must be full of rats."

Father said nothing. Instead he pushed back his chair and, going to the large cupboard where he kept some of his shooting things so that they would be available for after-work excursions, he swung wide the door and got out his gun case. He drew out the barrels, fore end, and stock and assembled the gun. He closed the breech and tried the triggers, and at that familiar sound Mutt was galvanized into life and came scuffling out from under the desk to stand with twitching nose and a perplexed air about him.

He had obviously been missing something. This wasn't the hunting season. But—the gun was out.

He whined interrogatively and my father patted his head. "Good boy," he said, and then walked to the screen door with Mutt crowding against his heels.

By this time the group of human watchers was as perplexed as Mutt. The six men stood in the office doorway and watched curiously as my father stepped out on the porch, raised the unloaded gun, leveled it down the alley toward the main street, pressed the triggers, and said in a quiet voice, "Bang—bang—go get 'em boy!"

To this day Father maintains a steadfast silence as to what his intentions really were. He will not say that he expected the result that followed, and he will not say that he did not expect it.

Mutt leaped from the stoop and fled down that alley-way at his best speed. They saw him turn the corner into the main street, almost causing two elderly women to collide with one another. The watchers saw the people on the far side of the street stop, turn to stare, and then stand as if petrified. But Mutt himself they could no longer see.

He was gone only about two minutes, but to the group upon the library steps it must have seemed much longer. The man from New York had just cleared his throat preparatory to a new and even more amusing sally, when he saw something that made the words catch in his gullet.

They all saw it—and they did not believe.

Mutt was coming back up the alley. He was trotting. His head and tail were high—and in his mouth was a magnificent ruffed grouse. He came up the porch stairs nonchalantly, laid the bird down at my father's feet, and with a satisfied sigh crawled back under the desk.

There was silence except for Mutt's panting. Then one of the local men stepped forward as if in a dream, and picked up the bird.

"Already stuffed, by God!" he said, and his voice was hardly more than a whisper.

It was then that the clerk from Ashbridge's Hardware arrived. The clerk was disheveled and mad. He came bounding up the library steps, accosted Father angrily, and cried:

"That damn dog of yours—you ought to keep him locked up. Come bustin' into the shop a moment ago and snatched the stuffed grouse right out of the window. Mr. Ashbridge's fit to be tied. Was the best bird in his whole collection. ..."

Mutt Makes His Mark

I do not know if the man from New York ever paid his debt. I do know that the story of that day's happening passed into the nation's history, for the Canadian press picked it up from the *Star-Phoenix*, and Mutt's fame was carried from coast to coast across the land.

That surely was no more than his due.

7

Battle Tactics

AFTER several years in Saskatoon, my family moved into a new neighborhood. River Road was on the banks of the Saskatchewan River, but on the lower and more plebian side. The community on River Road was considerably relaxed in character and there was a good deal of tolerance for individual idiosyncrasies.

Only three doors down the street from us lived a retired school-teacher who had spent years in Alaska and who had brought with him into retirement a team of Alaskan Huskies. These were magnificent dogs that commanded respect not only from the local canine population but from the human one as well. Three of them once caught a burglar on their master's premises, and they reduced him to butcher's meat with a dispatch that we youngsters much admired.

Across the alley from us lived a barber who maintained a sort of Transient's Rest for stray mongrels. There was an unkind rumor to the effect that he encouraged these strays only in order to practice his trade upon them. The rumor gained stature from the indisputable fact that some of his oddly assorted collection of dogs sported unusual haircuts. I came to know the barber intimately during the years that followed, and he confided his secret to me. Once, many years earlier, he had seen a French poodle shaven and shorn, and he had been convinced that he could devise even more spectacular hair styles for dogs, and perhaps make a fortune and a reputation for himself. His experiments were not without artistic merit, even though some of them resulted in visits from the Humane Society inspectors.

I had no trouble fitting myself into this new community, but the adjustment was not so simple for Mutt. The canine population of River Road was enormous. Mutt had to come to terms with these dogs, and he found the going hard. His long, silken hair and his fine "feathers" tended to give him a soft and sentimental look that was misleading and that seemed to goad the roughneck local dogs into active hostility. They usually went about in packs, and the largest pack was led by a well-built bull terrier who lived next door to us. Mutt, who was never a joiner, preferred to go his way alone, and this made him particularly suspect by the other dogs. They began to lay for him.

He was not by nature the fighting kind. In all his life I never knew him to engage in battle unless there was no alternative. His was an eminently civilized attitude, but one that other dogs could seldom understand. They taunted him because of it.

His pacific attitude used to embarrass my mother when the two of them happened to encounter a belligerent strange dog while they were out walking. Mutt would waste no time in idle braggadocio. At first glimpse of the stranger he would insinuate himself under Mother's skirt and no amount of physical force, nor scathing comment, could budge him from this sanctuary. Often the strange dog would not realize that it *was* a sanctuary and this was sometimes rather hard on Mother.

Despite his repugnance toward fighting, Mutt was no coward, nor was he unable to defend himself. He had his own ideas about how to fight, ideas which were unique but formidable. Just how efficacious they actually were was demonstrated to us all within a week of our arrival at our new address.

Knowing nothing of the neighborhood, Mutt dared to go where even bulldogs feared to tread, and one morning he foolishly pursued a cat into the ex-schoolteacher's yard. He was immediately surrounded by four ravening Huskies. They were a merciless lot, and they closed in for the kill.

Mutt saw at once that this time he would have to fight. With one quick motion he flung himself over on his back and began to pedal furiously with all four feet. It looked rather as if he were riding a bicycle built for two, but upside down. He also began to sound his siren. This was a noise he made—just how, I do not know—deep in the back of his throat. It was a kind of frenzied wail. The siren rose in pitch and volume as his legs increased their RPM, until he began to sound like a gas turbine at full throttle.

The effect of this unorthodox behavior on the four Huskies was to bring them to an abrupt halt. Their ears went forward and their tails uncurled as a look of pained bewilderment wrinkled their brows. And then slowly, and one by one, they began to back away, their eyes uneasily averted from the distressing spectacle before them. When they were ten feet from Mutt they turned as one dog and fled without dignity for their own back yard.

The mere sight of Mutt's bicycle tactics (as we referred to them) was usually sufficient to avert bloodshed, but on occasion a foolhardy dog would refuse to be intimidated. The results in these cases could be rather frightful, for Mutt's queer posture of defense was not all empty bombast.

Once when we were out hunting gophers Mutt was attacked by a farm collie who, I think, was slightly mad. He looked mad, for he had one white eye and one blue one, and the combination gave him a maniac expression. And he acted mad, for he flung himself on the inverted Mutt without the slightest hesitation.

Mutt grunted when the collie came down on top of him, and for an instant the tempo of his legs was slowed. Then he exerted himself and, as it were, put on a sprint. The collie became air-borne, bouncing up and down as a rubber ball bounces on the end of a water jet. Each time he came down he was raked fore and aft by four sets of rapidly moving claws, and when he finally fell clear he was bleeding from a dozen ugly scratches, and he had had a bellyful. He fled. Mutt did not pursue him; he was magnanimous in victory.

Had he been willing to engage deliberately in a few such duels with the neighborhood dogs, Mutt would undoubtedly have won their quick acceptance. But such was his belief in the principles of nonviolence—as these applied to other dogs, at least—that he continued to avoid combat.

The local packs, and particularly the one led by the bull terrier next door, spared no pains to bring him to battle, and for some time he was forced to stay very close to home unless he was accompanied by Mother or by myself. It was nearly a month before he found a solution to this problem.

The solution he eventually adopted was typical of him.

Almost all the back yards in Saskatoon were fenced with vertical planking nailed to horizontal two-by-fours. The upper two-by-four in each case was usually five or six feet above the ground, and about five inches below the projecting tops of the upright planks. For generations these elevated gangways had provided a safe thoroughfare for cats. One fine day Mutt decided that they could serve him too.

I was brushing my teeth after breakfast when I heard Mutt give a yelp of pain and I went at once to the window and looked out. I was in time to see him laboriously clamber up on our back fence from a garbage pail that stood by the yard gate. As I watched he wobbled a few steps along the upper two-by-four, lost his balance, and fell off. Undaunted he returned at once to the garbage pail and tried again.

I went outside and tried to reason with him, but he ignored me. When I left he was still at it, climbing up, staggering along for a few feet, then falling off again.

I mentioned this new interest of his during dinner that night, but none of us gave it much thought. We were used to Mutt's peculiarities, and we had no suspicion that there was method behind this apparent foolishness. Yet method there was, as I discovered a few evenings later.

The Dog Who Wouldn't Be

A squad of Bengal lancers, consisting of two of my friends and myself armed with spears made from bamboo fishing rods, had spent the afternoon riding up and down the back alleys on our bicycles hunting tigers (alley cats). As suppertime approached we were slowly pedaling our way homeward along the alley behind River Road when one of my chums, who was a little in the lead, gave a startled yelp and swerved his bike so that I crashed into him, and we fell together on the sun-baked dirt. I picked myself up and saw my friend pointing at the fence ahead of us. His eyes were big with disbelief.

The cause of the accident, and of my chum's incredulity, was nonchalantly picking his way along the top of the fence not fifty yards away. Behind that fence lay the home of the Huskies, and although we could not see them, we—and most of Saskatoon—could hear them. Their frenzied howls were punctuated by dull thudding sounds as they leaped at their tormentor and fell back helplessly to earth again.

Mutt never hesitated. He ambled along his aerial route with the leisurely insouciance of an old gentleman out for an evening stroll. The Huskies must have been wild with frustration, and I was grateful that the fence lay between them and us.

We three boys had not recovered from our initial surprise when a new canine contingent arrived upon the scene. It included six or seven of the local dogs (headed by the bull terrier) attracted to the scene by the yammering of the Huskies. They spotted Mutt, and the terrier immediately led a mass assault. He launched himself against the fence with such foolhardy violence that only a bull terrier could have survived the impact.

Battle Tactics

We were somewhat intimidated by the frenzy of all those dogs, and we lowered our spears to the "ready" position, undecided whether to attempt Mutt's rescue or not. In the event, we were not needed.

Mutt remained unperturbed, although this may have been only an illusion, resulting from the fact that he was concentrating so hard on his balancing act that he could spare no attention for his assailants. He moved along at a slow but steady pace, and having safely navigated the Huskies' fence, he jumped up to the slightly higher fence next door and stepped along it until he came to a garage. With a graceful leap he gained the garage roof, where he lay down for a few moments, ostensibly to rest, but actually—I am certain—to enjoy his triumph.

Below him there was pandemonium. I have never seen a dog so angry as that bull terrier was. Although the garage wall facing on the alley was a good eight feet high, the terrier kept hurling himself impotently against it until he must have been one large quivering bruise.

Mutt watched the performance for two or three minutes; then he stood up and with one insolent backward glance jumped down to the dividing fence between two houses, and ambled along it to the street front beyond.

The tumult in the alley subsided and the pack began to disperse. Most of the dogs must have realized that they would have to run halfway around the block to regain Mutt's trail, and by then he might be far away. Dispiritedly they began to drift off, until finally only the bull terrier remained. He was still hurling himself at the garage wall in a paroxysm of fury when I took myself home to tell of the wonders I had seen.

The Dog Who Wouldn't Be

From that day forth the dogs of the neighborhood gave up their attempts against Mutt and came to a tacit acceptance of him—all, that is, save the bull terrier. Perhaps his handball game against the fence had addled his brain, or it may be that he was just too stubborn to give up. At any rate he continued to lurk in ambush for Mutt, and Mutt continued to avoid him easily enough, until the early winter when the terrier—by now completely unbalanced—one day attempted to cross the street in pursuit of his enemy and without bothering to look for traffic. He was run over by an old Model T.

Mutt's remarkable skill as a fence walker could have led to the leadership of the neighborhood dogs, had that been what he desired, for his unique talent gave him a considerable edge in the popular game of catch-cat; but Mutt remained a lone walker, content to be left to his own devices.

He did not give up fence walking even when the original need had passed. He took a deep pride in his accomplishment, and he kept in practice. I used to show him off to my friends, and I was not above making small bets with strange boys about the abilities of my acrobatic dog. When I won, as I always did, I would reward Mutt with candy-coated gum. This was one of his favorite confections and he would chew away at a wad of it until the last vestige of mint flavor had vanished, whereupon he would swallow the tasteless remnant. Mother thought that this was bad for him, but as far as I know, it never had any adverse effect upon his digestive system, which could absorb most things with impunity.

8

Cats and Ladders

MUTT had always disliked cats, but until he became an expert fence walker, he had never been able to demonstrate his feelings in a truly efficient manner. The fenced-in back yards of Saskatoon might have been built to order for the cats, and specifically designed to thwart all dogs. Perhaps as a result of this favorable environment the cat population was large, and the cats themselves had grown careless and arrogant. It was understandable that they should feel this way, after many years of security; but it was a foolhardy attitude, as Mutt soon demonstrated.

Once he had perfected the art of fence walking, he became the scourge and often the nemesis of the cats on our block. When the surviving local cats became few in number, and wary, Mutt went farther afield, scouring alleys right across Saskatoon for cats that had not had warning of his unique abilities. Before the year was out he had engendered such a feeling of insecurity among the city's cats that they had become almost wholly arboreal.

Once having located a cat, Mutt would make the usual futile sort of dog rush in its direction. The cat would promptly climb the nearest fence and sit there feeling at ease and safe. With a dejected look Mutt would turn away, apparently accepting defeat, while the cat spat insults at his retreating back.

But having reached a corner of the fence, Mutt would turn suddenly and with a great leap gain the top two-by-four. Before the startled cat had time to stand its hair on end, Mutt would come rushing toward it, on its own level.

The cat would now find itself at a double disadvantage. It could not safely balance on the fence while it attempted to scratch out its assailant's eyes. Neither could it safely turn its back and flee. If it leaped down to the ground, it was at once in Mutt's native element. If it attempted to retreat along the fence, Mutt's long legs would soon catch it up. Only if there was a tree within instant reach could the cat hope to escape unscathed.

It was inevitable—Mutt being the way he was—that he would one day decide to follow his quarry into the upper branches. Nor was it as improbable an endeavor as it may sound. After all, there are many other terrestrial animals that occasionally take to the trees, and do so with some skill. Goats are often to be seen, in Mediterranean countries, browsing the upper branches of olive trees. Ground hogs will also climb trees, and there are many reports of coyotes having been treed by pursuing hounds.

Nevertheless, my family and I were electrified one morning to discover Mutt halfway up a tree in our back yard. He was climbing awkwardly but determinedly, and he got fifteen feet above the ground before a dead branch gave beneath his weight and he came bouncing down again. He was slightly bruised, and the

Cats and Ladders

wind was knocked out of him; but he had proved that climbing was not impossible for a dog, and from that moment he never looked down.

None of us realized just how far he would dare with his new skill until a day in the spring of the following year when a fire engine went streaking past our house with sirens blasting. I leaped aboard my bike and gave chase. Half a block from home I overtook a chum of mine named Abel Cullimore, also riding his bicycle, and I pulled up alongside to ask what the excitement was about.

Abel was a fat youth, and he was gasping for breath. "Don't know—for sure—" he panted. "I heard—wild animal—in a tree."

By this time we had turned down Seventh Avenue and we could see a small cluster of people grouped about the fire engine, which had stopped under a row of cottonwood trees a block ahead of us. The engine was a ladder truck and the ladder was extended so that its top was lost to view amidst the bright greenery above. As we drew near, a newspaper photographer stepped out of a car with his camera in his hand.

Two grim-looking householders were standing on the sidewalk beneath the cottonwoods, cradling shotguns in their arms. I walked over to them and, peering upward, caught a glimpse of familiar black and white fur, and I knew at once to whom it must belong.

Alarmed by the attitude of the two gunners, I hastened to explain to them that the thing up the tree was only a dog—*my* dog in fact.

This information was greeted with hostility.

"Smart-aleck kid!" one of the men remarked.

The other waved me away, saying sternly, "Run along, you boy. If you wasn't so young, I'd say you was corked."

The first man guffawed loudly, and I backed away. I could not really blame the men. The foliage was too thick for any stranger to identify the beast up in the tree, and anyway it was making a weird and most undoglike noise. Only Abel and I recognized the sounds as the plaintive chattering that Mutt made when he was in difficulties.

I was debating whether or not I dared accost the man who was operating the fire-truck controls when there came a startled cry from the branches overhead, into which a fireman armed with a gunny sack and a revolver had just disappeared.

"Son of a self-sealing cylinder," he bawled, a note of intense incredulity in his voice, "it's a damn dawg!"

Mutt and I were both greatly relieved when the fireman finally descended with the "dawg" slung over his shoulder. Mutt had suffered no harm, other than to his dignity, but that had been ruffled, and he slunk away for home the moment the fireman put him down.

Descending from trees always remained a difficulty for Mutt and when he began climbing ladders he encountered the same problem, and it got him into several curious situations.

His interest in ladders had followed naturally upon his tree-climbing experiments, and I encouraged him, for I was anxious to expand my renown as the owner of a remarkably acrobatic dog. We began with stepladders, and these were easy. Rung ladders

Cats and Ladders

followed, and before many days he could mount quickly and lightly to the roof of our house. But if the pitch of the ladder was at all steep, his attempts to descend, head first, degenerated into a free slide that ended with a thump on the ground below. Eventually he learned to control his descent by hooking his hind feet over progressively lower rungs, while he guided himself with his forefeet. But in the early stages of his ladder-climbing career he could only go up.

Not content to experiment with our ladders at home, Mutt would tackle any ladder he came across. It so happened that there lived on our street a man by the name of Couzinsky—a baker by trade, and on the night shift at his plant. It was Couzinsky's habit to spend the daylight hours improving the appearance of his two-story frame house. He used to repaint the entire house at least once a year, and each year he used a different color. One would have thought that he enjoyed ladder work almost as much as Mutt, for on any suitable day you could find Couzinsky perched high up under the eaves wielding his brush. He once explained his passion for painting in this way: "Why I painted? Why, you ask? She's lovely street, this place. Better I should look lovely too! And so I painted!"

And so he did.

I was not always fortunate enough to witness Mutt's misadventures, but I witnessed this one. It was unforgettable. It was on a Saturday afternoon and Mutt and I had been for a tramp along the riverbank looking for dinosaur bones. On the way home we passed Couzinsky's place and I noted with approval that he was changing his color scheme again, this time from green to puce. As I walked on I did not notice that Mutt was no longer at my heels, for I was engrossed in speculation about the possibility of finding dinosaur bones in the Anglican Church yard. By this, I hasten to explain, I mean that it had dawned on me that the gravediggers might conceivably stumble across such remains when they were about their work. I knew one of the diggers slightly, and I had just about decided that I would try to enlist his interest when there came a frightful shriek from somewhere behind me.

I spun on my heel and there, high on the south wall of Couzinsky's multicolored house, I saw a strange tableau.

At the very top of the ladder was Couzinsky himself. He was clinging by his hands to the eave trough, while from his right foot a gallon can of paint hung precariously suspended. Immediately below him was Mutt. Mutt's situation was most peculiar. He must have attempted to turn around on the upper rungs of the ladder, but he had only succeeded in thrusting his head and forequarters *through* the rungs so that he was balanced on his midriff and helpless to move in any direction. Couzinsky was still yelling fiercely, but Mutt was saving his breath.

I ran to their aid and, having clambered up the ladder, managed to get Mutt turned around. Couzinsky put his feet back on the top rung and we three descended to the ground.

As Mutt's nominal master I expected a severe dressing-down, but Couzinsky surprised me. Apparently his admiration for Mutt's climbing abilities outweighed the effects of the shock that he had suffered. It must have been a severe shock too.

Cats and Ladders

"I stand there painted," he explained to me, "'and no-where looking when it comes up between the legs. Dat dug! Oh my, dat dug! I yomp, what else?"

What else indeed. I only wonder that he did not yomp clear up onto the roof.

Mutt and I withdrew after I had made my apologies for both of us, and the outcome of the incident was that Couzinsky became our warmest friend in the neighborhood. He never tired of telling the story about "dat dug."

On another occasion Mutt found a tempting ladder, ascended it, and, being unable to turn around, simply clambered into an open second-story bedroom window and scratched at the closed bedroom door until the householder came upstairs and let him out. The owner of that house was another singular character. He had worked for the Canadian National Railways for thirty-odd years and as a result he was the most phlegmatic man I ever knew. Nothing could disturb his equanimity.

When he re-entered his living room after having let Mutt out the back door, his wife asked him what the noise upstairs had been, and he replied, "Nothing, my dear. Only a stray dog in the bedroom."

I know that this is true, for his wife told Mother about it during a tea party, and Mother, recognizing that the culprit must have been Mutt, told me.

It was after he had at last become fully competent at going both ways on a ladder that his brush with the Cat Lady occurred.

I never heard her other name, if indeed she had one. To all of us on River Road, adults and children alike, she was known only as the Cat Lady. She lived in a ramshackle frame house at the corner of our block, and she kept cats.

There must be many women like her in the world; spinsters, most of them, who suffer from frustration and who take to cats in compensation. Women of this kind can be truly formidable in their felinity, and such a one was our Cat Lady. She knew no other love, no other interest than her cats, and when she began to have differences with her neighbors and with the public-health authorities about them, she resolutely turned her back on the outer world. No human being was allowed to enter her house and for some ten years before we arrived on River Road, not even the milkman—a favored character whom she tolerated—had been inside her doors. She refused even to allow the meter readers to enter the basement, and finally the utility company had to cut off the power and the water.

No one had any accurate idea of how many cats her house actually contained. It was one of the entertainments of my friends and me to spy on the place—but circumspectly, for she was a devil with her tongue and with her broom—and count the cats that we could see on the windowsills. One Saturday I counted forty-eight, but a chum of mine swore that he had once counted sixty-five.

Because of dogs and neighbors, the cats were not allowed out into the yard, and the lower windows of the place were never opened, winter or summer. The interior of that house must have had an atmosphere reminiscent of the lion house at a second-rate zoo, for when the wind was right and the Cat Lady's upstairs windows were open, I could detect the unmistakable feline odor all the way down the block to our house.

In order to give her cats some opportunity for exercise the Cat Lady made use of an oddity in the design of her house. The place was built on a T plan with the crossbar representing a normal peak-roofed section facing on River Road, and the upright of the T representing a two-story structure with an almost flat roof that sloped gently toward the rear and terminated in a fifteen-foot drop to the back garden. Two gable windows of the main section of the house opened on to this flat-topped wing, and in fair weather these windows were opened and the cats could promenade over the roof to absorb fresh air and moonshine. They got no sunshine, for the Cat Lady allowed them no freedom in daylight, fearing perhaps that her neighbors would be able to make a sufficiently accurate count to force the public-health officials to take action.

I have no idea which one of us youths made the original suggestion. I was against it at first. It was only after much badinage, and many taunting reflections on my courage, and on Mutt's skill, that I consented.

There were five of us involved, and we chose a satisfactorily dark night toward the end of the summer holidays. We had no difficulty in transporting the ladder down the back alley and across the broken-down fence of the Cat Lady's property, and in setting it up against the end wall.

We had no difficulty with Mutt either. The cat smell was overwhelmingly powerful in his nostrils, and he, like the other dogs of the area, must have spent many a thoughtful hour considering ways and means of getting at this multitude of cats.

He went up the ladder with the quiet agility of a squirrel, but when he reached the roof his claws clattered alarmingly on the tin shingles. We discreetly retreated to the alley to await events.

Mutt encountered a cat almost at once. There was a sudden scurrying, a despairing squalling noise, and then a thud as something fell into the yard. At once the night grew hideous. There must have been a score of cats loose on the roof and in the darkness a frightful free-for-all began.

The Cat Lady lived in deathly fear of burglars, or at least of male intruders, and I suppose she immediately assumed the worst. There was a volume to her screams that the whole pack of Sabine women, taken all together, could hardly have bettered. I think there was also something else too, an ill-defined quality that seems to me now, looking back on it, to have expressed a kind of yearning hope.

We had not expected such a violent reaction and, appalled by it, we fled for the shelter of our respective homes, abandoning both Mutt and ladder. But I was smitten by conscience when only halfway home. I stopped and was trying to nerve myself to return to the scene, when Mutt happily caught up with me. He did not seem at all distressed; rather he seemed smugly self-satisfied, despite a four-pronged gash that ran the full length of his bulbous nose. From his point of view the evening had been a considerable success.

It was a success from everyone's point of view, except that of the poor Cat Lady—and, possibly, of the two policemen who shortly arrived upon the scene.

One of the policemen began to bang on the front door of the house, while the other raced around to the back in the hope of intercepting an escaping burglar. He found the ladder, but he had to fight his way up it against a perfect avalanche of cats that were hurriedly abandoning ship.

There was a brief account of the incident in the next day's paper, but Mutt received no recognition for the part that he had played. He would not have cared, had he known of this neglect. Throughout the next week he and the other local dogs had themselves a wonderful time hunting cats that had fled from the roof, or that had escaped when the police finally forced the front door of the Cat Lady's house.

Neither was justice visited upon us who were the instigators of the whole affair. The police concluded that "person or persons unknown" had attempted to break in, and had been foiled by prompt official action. The investigation was soon dropped since there were no helpful witnesses—all the Cat Lady's neighbors having sworn that they had seen nothing that might be of assistance to the police.

I have sometimes wondered about that. Only a week after the incident I received a brand-new and expensive .22 rifle as a gift from the man who lived next door to the Cat Lady, and to whom I had never even spoken before.

9

Concepcion and Misconception

ALTHOUGH our sojourn on the Saskatchewan plains satisfied my father in most respects, he nevertheless knew one hunger that the west could not still.

Before coming to Saskatoon he had always lived close to the open waters of the Great Lakes, and had been a sailor on them since his earliest days. Nor is this purely a figurative statement, for by his own account he was conceived on the placid waters of the Bay of Quinte—in a green canoe. He came by his passion for the water honestly.

During his first year in Saskatoon, he was able to stifle his nautical cravings beneath the weight of the many new experiences the west had to offer him; but during the long winter of the second prairie year, he began to dream. When he sat down to dinner of an evening he would be with Mother and myself in the flesh only, for in spirit he was dining on hardtack and salt beef on one of Nelson's ships. He took to carrying a piece of marlin in his pocket, and visitors to his office in the library would watch curiously as he tied and untied a variety of sailors' knots while talking in an abstracted voice about the problems of book distribution in prairie towns.

Knowing my father, and knowing too that he was not the kind to remain satisfied with a dream world, it came as no surprise to Mother and me when he announced that he intended to buy a ship and prove that a sailor could find fulfillment even on the drought-stricken western plains.

I was skeptical. Only the previous summer we had made a journey to Regina, the capital of the province, where I had spent some hours on the banks of Wascana Lake. Wascana was made by men, not God, and by just such men as my father. It boasted two yacht clubs and a fleet of a dozen sailing craft. But it could boast of no water at all. I have never seen anything as pitiful as those little vessels sitting forlornly on the sun-caked mud of the lake bottom, their seams gaping in the summer heat. I remembered Wascana when Father told us his plans and, supposing that he must remember the phantom lake as well, I asked him if he was contemplating dry-land sailing—on wheels perhaps?

I went to bed early, and without my supper. And I felt a little hurt, for I had only been trying to help.

He bought his ship a few weeks later. She was a sixteen-foot sailing canoe that, by some mischance, had drifted into the arid heart of Saskatchewan. Berthed temporarily in our basement, she looked small and fragile, but she was to prove herself a stout little vessel indeed, and in this year of 1957 she remains very much alive, still pert and active, and she and I still sail together every summer.

My father spent the balance of the winter laboring over her.

Concepcion and Misconception

With meticulous and loving care he built leeboards, splashboards, a mast, a steering oar, and a set of paddles. He borrowed Mother's sewing machine and made a sail out of the finest Egyptian cotton, shipped to him from Montreal. As for the canoe herself—he burnished her sides with steel wool, scraped them with glass, and painted and repainted until her flanks were as smooth as the surface of a mirror.

Then he applied the final coat of paint—bright green—and with some ceremony christened her *Concepcion*. He *said* that she was so named after an island in the Philippines.

Her launching took place on a day in early May. I helped Father carry her down to the riverbank beside the Twenty-fifth Street bridge and en route we collected an interested group of followers. Vessels of any sort had been unknown in Saskatoon since the time of the prairie schooners, and *Concepcion* was an eye-catching maiden in her own right.

As my father went about the task of stepping the mast and preparing the canoe for her first voyage, the crowd of onlookers increased steadily in numbers. High above our heads the ramparts of the bridge darkened with a frieze of spectators. They were all very quiet and very solemn as Father nodded his head to tell me that he was ready, and then I pushed *Concepcion* into her own element.

It was early spring and the Saskatchewan River was still in flood. My father knew all there was to know about water (so he believed) and it had not occurred to him that there would be much difference between the Bay of Quinte and the South Saskatchewan. There was a good breeze blowing and it riffled the surging brown surface of the water, effectively concealing the telltale swirls and vortexes beneath. The watchers on the bridge, on the other hand, knew a good deal about the nature of prairie rivers in the spring, and there may have been something funereal about the hush that lay upon them as they watched Father and *Concepcion* take to the stream.

The launching took place several hundred feet above the bridge, but by the time Father had everything shipshape, and was able to raise his eyes to look about, the bridge had inexplicably changed its position in relation to him. It was now several hundred yards behind him, and receding at a positively terrifying rate of speed. He became extremely active. He ran up the sail and began hauling in the sheet in an effort to come about.

From the parapets, where I now stood watching with the rest, there came a gasp of mingled awe and admiration. Most of the watchers had never seen a sailing vessel before and they had always understood that sail was an old-fashioned and painfully slow way of getting about. Their eyes were being opened.

Concepcion was acting strangely. She would not come about, for the current was stronger than the breeze. She resolutely skittered downstream, making about twelve knots. She should not have been making five in that light air, and my father knew it. He began to understand about the current. He got out his paddle and with almost demoniac frenzy strove to bring her head upstream. He was successful in the end, but by that time he and *Concepcion* were no more than a rapidly diminishing dot upon the distant surface of the river.

Concepcion and Misconception

Some of the men standing on the bridge beside me began making bets as to when Father would reach the town of Prince Albert, some hundreds of miles downstream. But it was clear that my father did not really want to reach Prince Albert. He was sailing the canoe now with a grim determination and a skill that he had probably never before been called upon to use. He wanted very badly to come back to Saskatoon.

Concepcion beat back and forth across the river like a wood chip on a frothing millrace. She tacked and beat, and though she kept her head resolutely upstream —and though she was sailing like a witch—she nevertheless kept diminishing in our view until at last she vanished altogether in the bright distance to the north.

One of the men near me glanced at his watch and spoke to his companion. "Eleven o'clock. 'Course, he'll be a mite slower now, goin' backward that way, but I reckon he'll hit the Prince Albert bridge by suppertime. I'll lay you fifty cents he does."

He would have lost his bet, however, for Father and *Concepcion* did not go to Prince Albert after all. They might have done so had they not been fortunate enough to run aground some ten miles below Saskatoon. Shortly after midnight they arrived home together, in a farm cart that was being towed by two noncommittal horses.

The setback to my father's design was only temporary. "Never mind," he said at breakfast the next day. "Wait till the spring flood passes, and *then* we'll see."

But what we saw when the flood was gone was not encouraging. The South Saskatchewan was back to normal, and normal consisted of a desert expanse of mud bars with here and there an expiring pool of trapped brown scum and, in a few very favored places, a sluggish trickle of moving water.

It was a sight that would have discouraged any man except my father. He refused to be defeated. He had made his plans, and the river would simply have to conform to them. That was the way he was.

His plans suited me well enough, for we closed up our rented house and moved our old caravan some ten miles south of the city to the Saskatoon Golf and Country Club. Here, on the wooded banks of the Saskatchewan, we established our summer residence.

It was a fine place for a boy to spend a summer. There were enough pools remaining in the river bed to provide swimming of a sort. There was a stretch of virgin prairie where coyotes denned and where determined gentlemen batted golf balls into gopher holes. And only a few miles away there was an Indian reservation.

My time was my own, for the summer holidays had begun, but my father had to commute to work in the city every day. He might easily have done so by car, but he had *planned* to commute by water and he refused to be dissuaded by the unco-operativeness of nature.

At seven o'clock on the first Monday morning he and *Concepcion* set out bravely, and full of confidence in one another. But when they returned late that evening, it was as passengers in, and on, a friend's automobile. My father was very weary; and uncommunicative about the day's adventures. It was not until years later that he admitted to me that he had actually walked eight of the ten miles to Saskatoon, towing *Concepcion* behind him through the shallows, or carrying her on his shoulders across sand bars. There had been a brief but exciting interlude with one sand bar that turned out to be quicksand, too, but on this he would not dwell.

Through the next few days he wisely, but reluctantly, commuted in Eardlie, but then there was a rainfall somewhere to the south and the river rose a few inches. Eardlie was again abandoned, and *Concepcion* returned to a place of favor. During the weeks that followed she and Father became intimately familiar with the multitudes of sand bars, the quicksands, and the other mysteries of the shrunken river's channels. And to the astonishment of all observers, my father began to make a success of his water route to the office. It was true that he still walked almost as far as he was able to paddle, but at least he was spared the ignominy of having to haul the canoe along in front of an audience, for a relatively deep channel running through the city enabled him to paddle the final mile of his route to the landing place near the Bessborough Hotel, with Hiawathan dignity.

He would not leave *Concepcion* on the riverbank to await his return, but carried her with him right to the library building. The first few times that he came trotting through the morning traffic in the city center with the green canoe balanced gracefully on his shoulders he caused some comment among the passers-by. But after a week or two people ceased to stare at him and no one, with the exception of a few ultraconservative ice-wagon horses, so much as gave him a second glance. He and *Concepcion* had become an unremarked part of the local scene.

The Dog Who Wouldn't Be

Mutt often accompanied Father and *Concepcion* down-river. He quickly developed the requisite sense of balance and would stand in the bow, his paws on the narrow foredeck, poised like a genuine gargoyle. This was not mere posturing on his part either, for he had taken it on himself to give warning when the canoe approached shallow water, or a hidden bar. His efficiency as a pilot was not high, despite his good intentions, for he was notoriously shortsighted. Nor could he, as they say, "read water." After a hysterical outburst prompted by a current boil that he had mistaken for a submerged log, he would very likely be staring placidly into space when *Concepcion* ran hard aground. If the canoe was traveling at any speed Mutt would be catapulted overboard to land on his face in the muddy water. He took such mishaps in good part, and would return to his piloting duties with increased vigilance.

Father was able to paddle *Concepcion* (more or less) on the river, but that mean-natured trickle gave him no opportunity to sail. Since it was sailing he really craved, he was forced to look for other waters, and one week end he announced that he would visit Manitou Lake—a vast saline slough that lies some hundred miles from Saskatoon.

Manitou is one of the saltiest bodies of water in the world and *Concepcion* was not designed to float in a medium that was hardly more fluid than molasses. She would have no part of Manitou. When we launched her, she hardly wet her keel, but sat on the surface of the lake like a duck upon a slab of ice.

My father was annoyed by her behavior and set about forcing his will upon her by loading her with rocks. It took an unbelievable number of boulders to force her down to her marks, and when Father and I finally clambered aboard, it was to find her about as maneuverable as a concrete coffin floating in gelatin. The water in which she stuck was so thick with salt that I could almost hear the stuff rasping on her sleek sides. And when we hoisted the sail, the wind had as little effect upon her as it would have had upon the Carnegie-built walls of the Saskatoon Public Library itself.

My father was infuriated by *Concepcion's* lack of response, and unwisely began to jettison the ballast. He had heaved half a dozen large boulders overside when the canoe decided she had had enough. One gunwale rose buoyantly while the other sank, and in short seconds we were floating on a serene sea, while below us *Concepcion* was slowly dragged toward the bottom by her bellyful of stone.

We were in no danger. It was physically impossible for an unweighted human body to sink in Manitou Lake. On the contrary, we rode so high out of the water that we had trouble navigating to the nearby shore. And when we came to salvaging *Concepcion*, who lay in some ten feet of water, the unnatural qualities of Manitou posed a serious problem. We found that we simply could not dive. It was a most eerie experience, for we could not force ourselves more than a foot below the surface. In the end, Father had to weight himself—like a South Sea pearl diver—with a basket full of stones. Clinging to this with one hand, he managed to reach the sunken ship and fasten a line to a thwart. Then he rather thoughtlessly let go of the basket. He came up from the depths like a playful salmon leaping after a fly, shot half out of the water, and fell back with a resounding thwack that must have hurt him as much as had *Concepcion's* behavior.

But, in the end, the frustrations which beset my father's desire to sail again were no match for his perseverance. In August of that memorable year we hitched the caravan to Eardlie, placed *Concepcion* on the roof, and went off on a dogged search for sailing waters. And we found them. Far to the north, in the jack-pine country beyond Prince Albert, we came to a place called Emma Lake, and it was an honest lake, filled with honest water, and caressed by amiable winds.

We launched *Concepcion* with trepidation—for there had been so many unfortunate episodes in the past. Then we climbed aboard, and hoisted sail.

It was the kind of day that graces the western plains, and only them. The sky was crystalline and limitless, and the hard sun cut the surface of the lake into a myriad of brilliant shards. Flocks of black terns swirled in the westerly breeze that came down on us from the pine forests and gently filled *Concepcion's* sail, bellowing it into a curve as beautiful as any wing. She came alive.

We sailed that day—all of it, until the sun went sickly behind the blue shield of smoke from distant forest fires, and sank away taking the breeze with it. And we sailed aboard a little ship whose swift and delicate motion was more than sufficient reward for the rebuffs that we had suffered.

10

The Cruise of *The Coot*

MY FATHER was not the only man in Saskatoon to know the frustrations and hungers of a landlocked sailor. There were a good many other expatriates from broad waters in the city, and he came to know most of them through his work, for on the library shelves was one of the finest collections of boating books extant. Some of my father's staff—who did not know a boat from a bloat—were inclined to take a jaundiced view of the nautical flavor of the annual book-purchase list, but, after all, he *was* the chief librarian.

Aaron Poole was one of those who appreciated my father's salted taste in books. Aaron was a withered and eagle-featured little man who had emigrated from the Maritime Provinces some thirty years earlier and who, for twenty-nine years, had been hungering for the sound and feel of salt water under a vessel's keel. The fact that he had originally come from the interior of New Brunswick and had never actually been to sea in anything larger than a rowboat during his maritime years was not relevant to the way Aaron felt. As a Maritimer, exiled on the prairies, he believed himself to be of one blood with the famous seamen of the North

Atlantic ports; and in twenty-nine years a man can remember a good many things that ought to have happened. Aaron's memory was so excellent that he could talk for hours of the times when he had sailed out of Lunenburg for the Grand Banks, first as a cabin boy, then as an able-bodied seaman, then as mate, and finally as skipper of the smartest fishing schooner on the coast.

Aaron's desire to return to the sea grew as the years passed, and finally in 1926, when he was in his sixty-fifth year, he resolved his yearnings into action and began to build himself a vessel. He married off his daughters, sold his business, sent his wife to California, and got down to work at something that really mattered. He planned to sail his ship from Saskatoon to New Brunswick—and he intended to sail every inch of the way. He was of that dogged breed who will admit no obstacles—not even geographical ones like the two thousand miles of solid land which intervened between him and his goal.

He designed his ship himself, and then turned the basement of his house on Fifth Avenue into a boat works. Almost as soon as her keel was laid, some well-meaning friend pointed out to Aaron that he would never be able to get the completed ship out of that basement—but Aaron refused to be perturbed by problems which lay so far in the future.

By the time we arrived in Saskatoon, Aaron and his boat had been a standing jest for years. Her name alone was still enough to provoke chuckles in the beer parlors, even among those who had already laughed at the same joke a hundred times. It was indicative of Aaron's singular disdain for the multitudes that he had decided to name his ship *The Coot.*

"What's the matter with *that*?" he would cry in his high-pitched and querulous voice. "Hell of a smart bird, the coot. Knows when to dive. Knows when to swim. Can't fly worth a hoot? Who the hell wants to fly a boat?"

Aaron's tongue was almost as rough as his carpentering, and that was pretty rough. He labored over his ship with infinite effort, but with almost no knowledge and with even less skill. Nor was he a patient man—and patience is an essential virtue in a ship-builder. It was to be expected that his vessel would be renamed by those who were privileged to see her being built. They called her *Putty Princess.*

It was appropriate enough. Few, if any, of her planks met their neighbors, except by merest chance. It was said that Blanding's Hardware—where Aaron bought his supplies—made much of its profit, during the years *The Coot* was a-building, from the sale of putty.

When my father and Aaron met, *The Coot* was as near completion as she was ever likely to get. She was twenty-four feet long, flat-bottomed, and with lines as hard and awkward as those of a harbor scow. She was hogged before she left her natal bed. She was fastened with iron screws that had begun to rust before she was even launched. The gaps and seams in her hull could swallow a gallon of putty a day, and never show a bit of it by the next morning.

Yet despite her manifold faults, she was a vessel—a ship—and the biggest ship Saskatoon had ever seen. Aaron could see no fault in her, and even my father, who was not blinded by a creator's love and who was aware of her dubious seaworthiness, refused to admit her shortcomings, because she had become a part of his dreams too.

Mother and I were expecting it, when one March day Father announced that he was taking a leave of absence from the library that coming summer, in order to help Aaron sail *The Coot* to Halifax.

Saskatoon took a keen interest in the project. Controversy as to *The Coot's* chances for a successful journey waxed furiously among the most diversified strata of society. The Chamber of Commerce hailed the venture with the optimism common to such organizations, predicting that this was the "Trail-Blazer step that would lead to Great Fleets of Cargo Barges using Mother Saskatchewan to carry Her Children's Grain to the Markets of the World." On the other hand, the officials of the two railroads made mock of *The Coot*, refusing to accept her as a competitive threat in the lucrative grain-carrying business.

But on the whole the city was proud that Saskatoon was to become the home port for a seagoing ship. Maps showing the vessel's route were published, together with commentaries on the scenic beauties that would meet the eyes of the crew along the way. It was clear from the maps that this would be one of the most unusual voyages ever attempted, not excluding Captain Cook's circumnavigation of the globe. For, in order to reach her destination, *The Coot* would have to travel northward down the South Saskatchewan to its juncture with the north branch, then eastward into Lake Winnipeg. From there the route would turn south to leave Manitoba's inland sea for the waters of the Red River of the North, and the territories of the United States. Continuing southward down the Minnesota River to St. Paul, *The Coot* would find herself in the headwaters of the Mississippi, and on that great stream would journey to the Gulf of Mexico. The rest of the trip would be quite straightforward—a simple sail around Florida and up the Atlantic Coast to the Gulf of St. Lawrence.

Sailing time (announced by banner headlines in the local paper—MOWAT AND POOLE TO SAIL WITH MORNING TIDE) was fixed for 8 A.M. on a Saturday in mid-June and the chosen point of departure was to be the mud flat which lies near the city's major sewer outlet on the river. The actual launching had to be postponed a day, however, when the ancient and gloomy prediction that Aaron would have trouble disentombing *The Coot* from his basement was found to be a true prophecy. In the end, a bulldozer had to be hired and Aaron, with the careless disdain of the true adventurer ordered the operator to rip out the entire east wall of his house so that *The Coot* might go free. The crowd which had gathered to see the launching, and which at first had been disappointed by the delay, went home that evening quite satisfied with this preliminary entertainment and ready for more.

Father and Aaron had reason to be thankful for the absence of an audience when they finally eased the vessel off the trailer and into the Saskatchewan. She made no pretense at all of being a surface ship. She sank at once into the bottom slime, where she lay gurgling as contentedly as an old buffalo in its favorite wallow.

The Dog Who Wouldn't Be

They dragged her reluctantly back on shore and then they worked the whole night through under the fitful glare of gasoline lanterns. By dawn they had recalked *The Coot* by introducing nine pounds of putty and a great number of cedar wedges into her capacious seams. They launched her again before breakfast—and this time she stayed afloat.

That Sunday morning the churches were all but deserted, and it was a gala crowd that lined the river shores to windward of the sewer. The mudbank was the scene of frantic activity. Father and Aaron dashed about shouting obscure orders in nautical parlance, and became increasingly exasperated with one another when these were misunderstood. *The Coot* waited peacefully, but there were those among us in the crowd of onlookers who felt that she hardly looked ready for her great adventure. Her deck was only partly completed. Her mast had not yet been stepped. Her rudder fittings had not arrived and the rudder hung uncertainly over the stern on pintles made of baling wire. But she was colorful, at least. In his hurry to have her ready for the launching, Aaron had not waited for the delivery of a shipment of special marine enamel, but had slapped on whatever remnants of paint he could find in the bottom of the cans that littered his workshop. The result was spectacular, but gaudy.

Both Aaron and Father had been the recipients of much well-meaning hospitality during the night, and by morning neither was really competent to deal with the technical problem of stowage. The mountain of supplies and gear which had accumulated on the mudbank would have required a whole flock of coots to carry it.

The Cruise of *The Coot*

Captain and mate bickered steadily, and this kept the crowd in a good humor as the hours advanced and the moment of departure seemed no nearer.

The patience of the onlookers was occasionally rewarded, as when Aaron lost control of a fifty-pound cheese—a gift from a local dairy—and it went spinning off into the flow from the sewer. The audience was entranced. Aaron danced up and down on the mud flat, shrilly ordering his mate to dive in and rescue the cheese, but the mate became openly mutinous, and the situation was only saved by the prompt action of two small boys armed with fishing poles who caught the truant cheese and steered it gently back to shore. They would not touch it with their hands, nor would anyone else, and long after *The Coot* had sailed, that cheese still sat on the mud flat, lonely and unloved.

Mutt was prominent during these proceedings. He had been signed on as ship's dog and the excitement attendant on the launching pleased him greatly. When willing hands finally pushed *The Coot* out into the stream, Mutt was poised on the foredeck, striking an attitude, and he was the first part of the deck cargo to go swimming when the overloaded vessel heeled sharply to starboard and shook herself free of her encumbrances.

The Coot came back to the mudbank once again. Mutt withdrew under the growing mountain of discarded supplies for which there was no room aboard the ship. It was not so much the sewer that had discomfited him, as it was the heartless laughter of the crowd.

Just before noon they sailed at last, and *The Coot* looked quite impressive as she swung broadside-to under the arches of the New

Bridge, accompanied by a flotilla of thirty-six sodden loaves of bread that had fallen through the bottom of a cardboard container which Aaron had retrieved from the wet bilges of the boat, and had incautiously set to dry upon the canted afterdeck.

Riding my bicycle along the shore path, I accompanied them for a mile before waving farewell and then returning to the city, where, with the rest of Saskatoon, I settled down to await reports of *The Coot's* progress.

Our newspaper had outdone itself to cover the story properly, for it had enrolled all the ferrymen along the river as special correspondents. The ferries were located every dozen miles or so. They were square scows, fitted with submerged wooden vanes that could be turned at an angle to the current so that the water pressure on them would force the ferries back and forth across the river, guided and held on their courses by steel cables that were stretched from shore to shore just below the surface. The ferrymen were mostly farmers, with little knowledge of wider waters than their own river, so the newspaper representative who visited them (himself a fugitive from a seaport town) had given each of them a careful briefing on the proper manner in which to report commercial shipping.

When, for five full days after *The Coot* left us, there was not a single report from a ferryman, we began to worry a little. Then on Friday night the operator of the first ferry below the city—some fifteen miles away—telephoned the paper in a state of agitation to report an object—unidentifiable due to darkness—that had swept down upon him just before midnight and, after fouling the ferry cable, had vanished again to the sounds of a banjo, a howling dog, and a frightful outpouring of nautical bad language.

The mysterious object was presumed to be *The Coot*, but the reporter who was dispatched to that section of the river at dawn could find no trace of the vessel. He drove on down stream and at last encountered a Ukrainian family living high above the riverbank. The farmer could speak no English and his wife had only a little, but she did the best she could with what she had.

She admitted that she had certainly seen *something* that morning—and here she stopped and crossed herself. It had looked to her, she said, like an immense and garish coffin that could never have been intended for a mere human corpse. When she saw it first it was being hauled across a broad mud flat by—and she crossed herself again—a horse and a dog. It was accompanied, she continued, by two nude and prancing figures that might conceivably have been human, but were more likely devils. Water devils, she added after a moment's thought. No, she had not seen what had happened to the coffin. One glance had been enough, and she had hurried back into her house to say a prayer or two before the family icon—just in case.

The reporter descended to the river and there he found the marks left by the cortege in the soft mud. There were two sets of barefoot human tracks, a deep groove left by a vessel's keel, and one set each of dog and horse prints. The tracks meandered across the bar for two miles and then vanished at the edge of a navigable stretch of water. *All* the tracks vanished—including those of the horse. The reporter returned to Saskatoon with his story, but he had a queer look in his eye when he told us what he had seen.

As to what had actually happened during those five days when *The Coot* was lost to view, my father's log tells very little. It contains only such succinct and sometimes inscrutable entries as these: *Sun. 1240 hrs. Sink. Again. Damn. ... Sun. 2200 hrs. Putty all gone. Try mud. No good. ... Wed. 1600 hrs. A. shot duck for din., missed, hit cow. ... Thurs. 2330 hrs. Rud. gone west. Oh Hell! ... Fri. 1200 hrs. Thank God for Horse.*

But the story is there nevertheless.

It was in an amiable and buoyant mood that Father and Aaron saw the last of Saskatoon. That mood remained on them for three miles during which they made reasonably good progress, being forced to make for shore—before they sank—only four times. At each of these halts it was necessary to unload *The Coot* and turn her over to drain the water out. Aaron kept insisting that this would not be necessary in the future. "She'll soon take up," he told my father. "Wait till she's been afloat awhile."

As the day drew on, the initial mood of amity wore thin. "She'll take up all right," my father remarked bitterly as they unloaded *The Coot* for the twelfth time. "She'll take up the whole damned river before she's done—that's what she'll do!"

By the time they established their night camp they had covered a total distance of six miles, and *The Coot* had lost what little putty still remained in her. Her crew slept fitfully that night.

On Monday there was little difficulty keeping the water out, since there was no water—only a continuous sand bar. It was a terrestrial day, and they hauled *The Coot* the entire two miles that they made good before sunset. The three days which followed were of a similar nature. Mutt began to get footsore from sand between his toes. Because they spent so much of their time slithering and falling in the river muck as they attempted to haul *The Coot* a little farther on her way, both Father and Aaron abandoned clothing altogether and went back to nature.

They kept making new discoveries about their vessel and her equipment, and these were almost all discouraging. They found that in the monstrous pile of stores left behind in Saskatoon had been the fuel for the stove; the ammunition for the shotgun, though not (alas for an innocent cow) for the .22 rifle; the ax; and, blackest of all omissions, three bottles of Jamaica rum. They found that most of their soft rations were inedible because of prolonged immersion in sewage water, and they found that their sodden blankets were in an equally unsanitary state. They found that all the labels of the canned goods had washed away, and they discovered that the two cases of gleaming, but nameless, cans which they had supposed held pork and beans actually held dog food intended for Mutt.

I do not wonder that the log had so little to say about those days. I only wonder that *The Coot* continued on her voyage at all. But continue she did, and on Thursday evening her crew was rewarded by at last reaching relatively navigable waters. It was nearly dusk by then, but neither mate nor skipper (both of whom had become grim and uncommunicative) would be the first to suggest a halt, and Mutt had no say in the matter.

They pushed *The Coot* off the final sand bar and slipped away downstream into the darkness. At midnight they fouled the ferry cable, and lost their rudder.

That loss was not so serious as it seemed to them at the time, for before dawn they were aground again—and again trudging over the mudbanks with the towropes gnawing into their bare shoulders while *The Coot* obstinately dragged her keel.

They had paused for a while in order to cook a dismal breakfast when my father, happening to glance up at the high bank, saw the horse. Inspiration came to him and he leaped to his feet, shouting with elation. He was no longer shouting when, after hiking five miles over the burning prairie in order to find the horse's owner, and arrange for a temporary rental, he came wearily back down the banks of the river to rejoin *The Coot*. Aaron greeted him with unwonted joviality and a momentous announcement. "I've found it, Angus!" he cried, and held aloft one of the precious bottles which had been given up for lost.

It was the turning point of the journey.

By noon the amiable horse had dragged *The Coot* across the two-mile flats to open water once again. Aaron allowed the horse to wade a little way out from shore in order to float *The Coot*. He was about to halt the beast in order to untie the towrope when my father's genius renewed itself. "Why stop him now?" Father asked.

Aaron looked at his mate with growing affection, and passed the bottle. "By God, Angus," he said, "for a librarian you've got quite a brain."

So *The Coot* proceeded on her way under one horsepower and, since the river seldom was more than three feet deep, the horse experienced but little difficulty in his strange role. When, as occasionally happened, he struck a deep hole, he simply swam until he could touch bottom once again. And when the water shoaled into a new sand bar, *The Coot's* passengers jumped ashore and helped him haul.

The use of a river horse was a brilliant piece of improvisation, and it might well have sufficed to carry the voyagers to Lake Winnipeg—where they would assuredly have drowned—had it not been for the flood.

When the rain began on Saturday afternoon, Father and Aaron took *The Coot* to shore, hauled her a little way up the flats, covered her with a big tarpaulin, and crawled under the canvas to wait out the downpour. The horse was turned loose to scale the high banks and forage for himself, while the two men and the dog relaxed cozily in their shelter over tins of dog food and dollops of red rum.

The rain grew heavier, for it was the beginning of one of those frightening prairie phenomena—a real cloudburst. In less than three hours, three inches of water fell on the sun-hardened plains about Saskatoon and that was more than the total rainfall during the previous three months. The ground could not absorb it and the steep-sided gulches leading into the valley of the Saskatchewan began to roar angrily in spate. The river rose rapidly, growing yellow and furious as the flow increased.

The first crest of the flood reached *The Coot* at about five o'clock in the afternoon, and before her crew could emerge from their shelter, they were in mid-stream, and racing down the river at an appalling clip. Rudderless, and with only one remaining oar—for Aaron had used the other to support a tea pail over an open fire a few days earlier, and then had gone off to sit and think and had forgotten about oar, tea, and fire—there was nothing useful that *The Coot's* crew could do to help themselves. The rain still beat down upon them, and after a brief, stunned look at the fury of the river, they sensibly withdrew under their canvas hood, and passed the bottle.

By seven o'clock the rain had moderated to a steady drizzle, but the flood waters were still rising. In Saskatoon we who waited impatiently for news of *The Coot* were at last rewarded. The arrangements made by the newspaper began to bear fruit. Reports began arriving from ferrymen all down the river, and these succeeded one another so swiftly that at times they were almost continuous. The telephone exchange at the newspaper office was swamped with messages like this one:

SPECIAL TO THE STAR:

SAILING VESSEL, COOT, OUTBOUND IN BALLAST FROM SAS-KATOON, SIGHTED AT INDIAN CROSSING AT 7:43 P.M. ON COURSE FOR HALIFAX, THAT IS IF SHE DON'T GO BUSTING INTO THE BIG ISLAND BAR AFORE SHE GITS PAST COYOTE CREEK.

The Coot got by Big Island and Coyote Creek all right, for at 7:50 P.M. the watcher at Barners Ford reported that she had just passed him, accompanied by two drowned cows, also presumed to be en route for Halifax. At 8:02 she went by Indian Crossing ... at 8:16 she sideswiped the Sinkhole Ferry ... at 8:22 she was reported from St. Louis (Saskatchewan, not Missouri) ... and so it went. The ferrymen tried to "speak" the speeding ship, but she gave them no reply and would not even deign to make her number. So swiftly did she pass that a hard-riding stockman who spotted her near Duck Lake could not even draw alongside.

In the city room at the newspaper, reporters marked each new position on a large-scale map of the river, and someone with a slide rule calculated that if *The Coot* could maintain her rate of speed, she would complete her passage to Halifax in six more days.

By nine o'clock that evening the darkness of an overcast and moonless night had so obscured the river that no further reports were to be expected from the watching ferrymen. However, we presumed that on Sunday morning the observers would again pick up the trail. A number of people even drove out at dawn from Prince Albert to see *The Coot* go past the junction of the two branches of the river. They made that trip in vain. The flood passed and the river shrank back to its normal, indolent self, but no *Coot* appeared. She had vanished utterly during the black hours of the night.

All through that tense and weary Sunday we waited for news, and there was none. At last Aaron's son-in-law called on the Royal Canadian Mounted Police for help, and the famous force ordered one of its patrol aircraft up to make a search. The plane found nothing before darkness intervened on Sunday evening, but it was off again with the following dawn.

The Dog Who Wouldn't Be

At 11 A.M. on Monday the following radio message was received in Saskatoon:

COOT LOCATED FIVE MILES NORTHWEST FENTON AND TWO MILES FROM RIVERBANK. AGROUND IN CENTER LARGE PASTURE AND ENTIRELY SURROUNDED BY HOLSTEIN COWS. CREW APPEARS ALL WELL. ONE MAN PLAYING BANJO, ONE SUNBATHING, AND DOG CHASING CATTLE.

It was an admirable report, and indicative of the high standards of accuracy, combined with brevity, for which the force is justly famed. However, as my father later pointed out, it did not tell the entire story.

Mutt, Aaron, and Father had spent the whole of Saturday night under cover of their tarpaulin. Even after the rain stopped they did not emerge. Father said that this was because he wished to die bravely, and he could do so only by ignoring the terror and turmoil of that swollen river. Aaron said it was because they had found the second bottle of rum. Mutt, as usual, kept his peace.

When the light grew strong on Sunday morning, Father began to hope that they might yet survive and, pulling aside the canvas, thrust his head out for a look. He was stupefied by what he saw. *The Coot* had evidently managed to cover the entire distance to Lake Winnipeg in less than ten hours. His bemused mind could find no other explanation for the apparently limitless expanse of brown water that stretched away on every side.

It was not until later afternoon, when the flood waters began to subside and the tops of poplar trees began appearing alongside *The Coot*, that the illusion was partially dispelled. It had vanished totally by Monday morning when the voyagers awoke to find their vessel resting on a broad green meadow, surrounded by a herd of curious cattle.

The crew of *The Coot* now proceeded to enjoy the happiest hours of their journey. There was no water in the boat, or under her. There was no sand or mud. The sun was warm. Aaron had found the third of the missing bottles, and Father had procured a side of home-cured bacon and five loaves of homemade bread from a nearby Dukhobor settler. Mutt was having a time with the cows. It was a fair and lovely place for storm-tossed mariners to drop their hook.

The idyll was disturbed by the appearance of the search aircraft; and shattered a few hours later by the arrival of Aaron's son-in-law as a passenger in a big red truck. A conference was called and the cruise was declared to be at an end, despite Aaron's blasphemous dissent. *The Coot* went ignominiously back to Saskatoon aboard the truck.

When he was safely within his own house, Father frankly admitted to us that he was delighted to be there, and that he had never really had much hope of seeing home again. For the rest of that summer he was content with *Concepcion*, and we spent many a happy week end on Lotus Lake, sailing her back and forth between the Anglican Church Beach and Milford's Beach Parlour.

But there is a curious postscript to the story of *The Coot*. One day in the autumn of the following year my father received a letter from Halifax. It contained nothing save a snapshot which showed a funny little craft (unmistakably *The Coot*) tied up alongside that famous Lunenburger *The Bluenose*. On the back of the snapshot was a cryptic message, scrawled large in purple ink. "Quitter!" it said.

Father would have felt badly about that, had not his friend Don Chisholm (who was assistant superintendent of one of the railroads at Saskatoon) shown him a way-bill sometime earlier. It was an interesting document. It dealt with the dispatch of one flatcar, "with cargo, out of Saskatoon, bound for Halifax." And the name bestowed on that flatcar for the journey by some railway humorist was writ large on the bottom of the bill.

It was *The Cootie Carrier*.

11

Vignettes of Travel

THE MOWAT FAMILY was a restless one—or at least my father was a restless one. Mother would have been content to stay quietly in almost any of the places that were temporarily home to us, but Father always yearned for far horizons.

During the Saskatoon period of our lives we traveled widely, from Churchill on Hudson Bay, to Vancouver on the Pacific shores. We traveled the hard way, too, for a librarian is always underpaid. However, the lessons I learned from the vicissitudes of those journeys have stood me in good stead on my own travels, for writers too are always underpaid.

In examining my memories of those excursions I am struck by the way Mutt looms so large in all of them. There was our journey to the Pacific, for example. Looking back on it now, I can recall a string of vignettes in each of which Mutt was the center of attention—while for the rest, there is nothing but an amorphous blur.

We began that journey on the June day in 1934 when I finished my last school examination paper. I still possess a snapshot taken of us as we are pulled away down River Road, and when I look at it

The Dog Who Wouldn't Be

I am appalled at the manner in which we burdened Eardlie. None of your pregnant glass-and-chrome showcases of today could have carried that load for a single mile. Eardlie could do so only because he was the ultimate result of five thousand years of human striving to devise the perfect vehicle. For there is no doubt at all but that the Model A stands at the apex of the evolution of the wheel. And it is a matter of sorrow to me—as it should be to all men—that this magnificent climax should have been followed by the rapid and terrible degeneration of the automobile species into the effete mechanical incubi which batten off human flesh on every highway of the world today.

The load that Eardlie shouldered when he set bravely forth to carry us across far mountains to the sea almost defies belief. There was a large umbrella tent tied to the spare tire; there was *Concepcion* supported high above us on a flimsy rack; there were three folding wooden cots lashed to the front mudguards; on the right-hand running board (an invaluable invention, long since sacrificed to the obesity of the modern car) were two wooden crates of books—most of them about the sea; on the other running board were two trunk-suitcases, a five-gallon gasoline can, and a spare-tire. In addition, there were the canoe masts, sails, and lee-boards; Father's Newfoundland-pattern oilskins and sou'wester; a sextant; a schooner's binnacle compass; Mother's household implements, including pots and pans and a huge gunny sack containing shreds of cloth for use in making hooked rugs; and, not least, a canvas bag containing my gopher traps, .22 rifle, and other essential equipment.

Vignettes of Travel

As Eardlie arched his back under the strain and carried us out of the city past the town slough, where the ducks were already hatching their young, we would have done justice to Steinbeck's description of the dispossessed.

Mutt enjoyed traveling by car, but he was an unquiet passenger. He suffered from the delusion, common to dogs and small boys, that when he was looking out the right-hand side, he was probably missing something far more interesting on the left-hand side. In addition, he could never be quite sure whether he preferred the front seat—and looking forward—or the rumble seat—and looking backward. Mutt started out up front with Mother and Father, while I had the rumble seat; but we had not gone five miles before he and Mother were at odds with one another. They both wanted the outside berth, and whichever one was temporarily denied it would growl and mutter and push, until he or she gained his or her ends.

Before we had been driving for an hour Mother lost her patience and Mutt was exiled to the rumble seat.

Riding in the rumble did strange things to him, and I have a theory that his metabolism was disturbed by the enforced intake of air under pressure from the slip stream, so that he became oxygen drunk. He would grow wild-eyed and, although not normally a drooling dog, he would begin to salivate. Frequently he would stand up with his front feet on the back of Mother's neck, and he would drool on her until, driven to extremes, she would poke him sharply on the chin, whereupon he would mutter, and come back to drool on me.

But his favorite position, when he became really full of oxygen, was to extrude himself gradually over one of the rear mudguards until there was nothing of him remaining in the car except his hind feet and his tail. Here he would balance precariously, his nose thrust far out into the slip stream and his large ears fluttering in the breeze.

The prairie roads were indescribably dusty, and his nose and eyes would soon become so clogged that he would be almost blind, and incapable of smelling a dead cow at twenty paces. He did not seem to mind, but like a misshapen and misplaced figurehead he would thrust farther outward until he passed the point of balance. Then only my firm grip on his tail could prevent disaster, and on one occasion, when my grip relaxed a little, he became air-borne for a moment or so before crashing to the road behind us.

When this happened we thought we had lost him forever. By the time Father got the car stopped, Mutt was a hundred yards in the rear, spread-eagled in the center of the road, and screaming pitifully. Father assumed the worst, and concluded that the only thing to do was to put the poor beast out of his misery at once. He leaped out of the car and ran to a blacksmith's shop that stood by the roadside, and in a few minutes returned waving the blacksmith's old revolver.

He was too late. While he had been out of sight, Mutt had spotted a pair of heifers staring at him over the fence, and had hastily picked himself up to give vociferous chase.

Although he suffered no lasting injuries from this mishap, there was one minor consequence that allowed me to make a place for myself in the family annals by subsequently reporting that "Mutt was so scared he went to the bathroom in his pants."

[136]

Vignettes of Travel

Because of the dust we three human travelers were equipped with motorcyclists' goggles. Father decided one evening that this was favoritism, and that Mutt should have the same protection. We were then entering the outskirts of a place called Elbow, a typical prairie village with an unpaved main street as wide as the average Ontario farm, and with two rows of plank-fronted buildings facing each other distantly across this arid expanse. The drugstore was the only place still open when we arrived.

Father, Mutt, and I entered the shop together, and when an aged clerk appeared from the back premises, my father asked him for driving goggles.

The old fellow searched for a long time and finally brought us three pairs that had been designed and manufactured in the first years of the automobile era. They seemed to be serviceable and without more ado Father began trying them on Mutt.

Happening to glance up while this was going on, I met the clerk's gaze. He was transfixed. His leathered face had sagged like a wet chamois cloth and his tobacco-stained stubs seemed ready to fall from his receding lower jaw.

Father missed this preliminary display, but he was treated to an even better show a moment later when he got briskly to his feet, holding the second pair of goggles.

"These will do. How much are they?" he asked. And then suddenly remembering that he had forgotten to pack his shaving kit before leaving Saskatoon, he added, "We'll want a shaving brush, soap, and a safety razor too."

The old man had retreated behind his counter. He looked as if he was going to begin weeping. He pawed the air with one ema-ciated hand for several seconds before he spoke.

"Oh, Gawd!" he wailed—and it was a real prayer. "Don't you tell me that dawg *shaves*, too!"

We had to improvise a special harness for the goggles because of the unusual shape of Mutt's head, but they fitted him tolerably well, and he was pleased with them. When they were not in use we would push them up on the lift of his brow, but in a few days he had learned how to do this for himself, and he could put them down again over his eyes in time of need. Apart from the effect they had on unimaginative passers-by, Mutt's goggles were an unqualified success. However, they did not give him protection for his nose and one day he met a bee at forty miles an hour. The left side of Mutt's already bulbous nose swelled hugely. This did not inconvenience him too severely, for he simply moved to the other side of the car. But luck was against him and he soon collided with another bee, or perhaps it was a wasp this time. The total effect of the two stings was bizarre. With his goggles down, Mutt now looked like a cross between a hammer-head shark and a deep-sea diver.

Our second night on the western road was spent at Swift River in southern Saskatchewan. Swift River was almost the center of the dust-bowl country and it had a lean and hungry look. We were very hot, very dusty, and very tired when we drove into its northern outskirts and began searching for the municipal tourist camp—for in those times there were no motels and the only alternative to a tent of one's own was a tiny cubicle in a crematorium that bore the sardonic title of "hotel."

Vignettes of Travel

Swift River was proud of its municipal tourist camp, which was located in a brave but pathetic attempt at a park, near the banks of an artificial slough.

We set about pitching the tent, which was a patented affair and not easily mastered. Soon a policeman came along and eyed us suspiciously, as if convinced that we were undesirable vagrants masquerading as bona fide tourists. He became quite grumpy when called upon to help with the tent.

We were all in a taut temper when we finally crawled into our blankets that night. It did not ease our mood that the night's rest was fragmentary due to the influx of clouds of mosquitoes from the nearby slough, and due also to the sad moanings of a pair of emaciated elk who lived in a nearby wildlife enclosure.

We tossed and muttered in the hot and crowded tent, and were not disposed to rise with the dawn. We were still abed, still partly comatose, when voices near at hand brought us unwilling back to the new day.

The voices were feminine, spinsterish, and indignant. I was too drugged with fatigue to catch the gist of the conversation at first, but I was sufficiently conscious to hear Father's sudden grunt of anger, and Mother's whispered attempts to soothe him. Things seemed interesting enough to warrant waking fully, so I sat up in bed and gave the voices my attention.

The dialogue went like this:

From outside: "It's a shame—that's what it is. A regular public nuisance! I can't imagine what the officials are thinking of to allow it."

Mutterings from Father, who seemed to know what this was all about: "Old harridans! Who the devil do they think they are?"

Mother, soothingly: "Now, Angus!"

Outside again: "What a perfectly *poisonous* smell. ... Do you think it really *is* a dog?"

At this my father jerked convulsively, and I remembered that Mutt had abandoned the dubious comforts of the tent in the early dawn and had walked over me, seeking the doorway. I began to share my father's annoyance. No strangers had the right to speak of Mutt in terms like these. And they were growing worse.

"It looks like a dog—but how it stinks!" the disembodied and waspish voice continued. "Phew! Whoever owns it should be put in jail."

This was more than Father could bear. His bellow shook the tent.

"I *own* that dog," he cried, "and what do you intend to do about it?"

He had already begun to stumble about, looking for his clothes, when one of the voices responded in a manner that unhinged him completely.

"Well!" it said scathingly. "Why don't you bury it—or is that too much to expect from—from drifters!"

It was at this point that Father burst out of the tent, clad only in his pajama tops, and so angry that he was incoherent. Wordless he may have been, but his tone of voice was sufficient to send the two bird watchers—for that is what they were—skittering to their car. They vanished with a clash of gears, leaving us alone with the unhappy elk—and with a dog.

Vignettes of Travel

It was not Mutt. It was a strange dog, and it floated belly up in a backwater of the slough not more than twenty feet away. It had been dead a long, long time.

Mother was triumphant. "There, you see," she told my father. "You never *look* before you leap."

She was undeniably right, for if Father had looked we would have been spared the half hour that followed when the grumpy policeman returned and demanded that we haul our dog out of the slough and bury it at once. He was really more truculent than grumpy, and he did not have a sympathetic ear for our attempts at explanation. It would perhaps have been easier to convince him that the whole affair was a misunderstanding had Mutt been present, but Mutt had gone off in the early dawn to examine the quality of Swift River's garbage cans, and he did not return until Eardlie stood packed and ready to flee. Mutt never understood why Father was so short with him for the rest of the day.

The remainder of our journey through the prairies passed without undue excitement, and this was well, for it was a time of mounting fatigue, and of tempers strained by days of heat, by the long pall of dust, and by the yellowed desert of the drying plains. The poplar bluffs were few and far between, and their parched leaves rustled stiffly with the sound of death. The sloughs were dry, their white beds glittering in the destroying heat. Here and there a tiny puddle of muck still lingered in a roadside ditch, and these potholes had become death traps for innumerable little families of ducks. Botulism throve in the stagnant slime, and the ducks died in their thousands, and their bodies did not rot, but dried as mummies dry.

It was a grim passage, and we drove Eardlie hard, heedless of his steadily boiling radiator and his laboring engine. And then one morning there was a change. The sky that had been dust hazed for so long grew clear and sweet. Ahead of us, hung between land and air, we saw the first blue shadows of the distant mountains.

We camped early that night and we were in high spirits at our escape from drought and desert. When the little gasoline stove had hissed into life and Mother was preparing supper, Mutt and I went off to explore this new and living land. Magpies rose ahead of us, their long tails iridescent in the setting sun. Pipits climbed the crests of the high clouds and sang their intense little songs. Prairie chickens rose chuckling out of a green pasture that lay behind a trim white farmhouse. We walked back to the tent through a poplar bluff whose leaves flickered and whispered as live leaves should.

We crossed through most of Alberta the next day, and by evening were climbing the foothills. It had been a day for Mutt to remember. Never had he suspected that cows existed anywhere in such vast numbers. The size of the herds bewildered him so much that he lost all heart for the chase. He was so overwhelmed (and so greatly outnumbered) that he stayed in the car even when we stopped for lunch. In the evening we made our camp near a little roadside stand that sold gasoline and soda pop, and here Mutt tried to recover his self-respect by pursuing a very small, very lonely little cow that lived behind the garage. His cup of woe was filled to overflowing when the little cow turned out to be a billy goat—Mutt's first—and retaliated by chasing him back to the tent, and then attempting to follow him inside.

We began the passage of the mountains in the morning, and we chose the northern route, which at that time was no easy path even for a Model A. The roads were narrow, precipitous, and gravel surfaced. There were no guard rails, and periodically we would find ourselves staring over the edge of a great gorge while Eardlie's wheels kicked gravel down into the echoing abyss.

We seemed to undergo a strange shrinking process as the mountains grew higher and more massive. I felt that we were no more than four microorganisms, dwarfed almost to the vanishing point. The mountains frightened me, because I knew them as the last of the Terrible Things—the immutable survivors that alone remained unaltered by the human termites who have scarred the face of half a world.

Mutt too was humbled at first, and he showed his awe of the mountains in an odd way. He refused to use them for mundane purposes, and since there was nowhere else to cock a leg, except against a mountain, he was in agony for a time. Fortunately for him his awe was transitory. It was eventually replaced by the urge to climb, for the desire to seek high places had always been his, and it had taken him first to the top of fences, then up ladders, and finally high into the trees. Now he saw that it could take him to the clouds, and he was no dog to miss an opportunity.

We lost Mutt, and two days from our itinerary, when he set out on his own to reach the peaks of the Three Sisters. We never knew for certain if he achieved his goal, but when he arrived back at our impatient camp, his paw pads were worn almost to the flesh and he had a cocky air about him as of one who has stood upon a pinnacle and gazed across the world.

This mountain-climbing passion was an infernal nuisance to the rest of us, for he would sneak away whenever we stopped, and would appear high on the face of some sheer cliff, working his way steadily upward, and deaf to our commands that he return at once.

One day we paused for a drink of spring water near the face of a forbidding cliff, and of course Mutt was unable to resist the challenge. We did not notice that he was gone until a large American limousine drew up alongside us and from it four handsome women and two well-fed men emerged. They were all equipped with movie cameras and binoculars, and some of them began staring at the cliff with their glasses, while the rest leveled their cameras. The whirr of the machines brought me over to see what this was all about. I asked one of the women.

"Hush, sonny," she replied in a heavy whisper, "there's a real live mountain goat up there!" And with that she too raised her camera and pressed the button.

I spent a long time looking for that goat. I could see Mutt clearly enough, some three hundred feet up the cliffside; but no goat. I supposed that Mutt was on the goat's trail, and it irked me that I was blind while these strangers were possessed of such keen eyes.

After some ten minutes of intent photography the Americans loaded themselves back into the limousine and drove away, engaging in much congratulatory backslapping at their good luck as they went.

I had caught on by then. That night we discussed the anomaly of a piebald mountain goat with long black ears, and I am afraid we laughed outrageously. Yet in point of fact no genuine mountain goat could have given a more inspired demonstration of mountaineering techniques than could Mutt.

Leaving the mountains temporarily, we descended into the Okanagan valley, where we hoped to see a fabulous monster called the Ogo Pogo that dwells in Lake Okanagan. The monster proved reluctant, so we solaced ourselves by gorging on the magnificent fruits for which the valley is famous, and for which we had often yearned during the prairie years. To our surprise—for he could still surprise us on occasion—Mutt shared our appetites, and for three days he ate nothing at all but fruit.

He preferred peaches, muskmelon, and cherries, but cherries were his undoubted favorites. At first he had trouble with the pits, but he soon perfected a rather disgusting trick of squirting them out between his front teeth away from us and the car whenever he was eating cherries.

I shall never forget the baleful quality of the look directed at Mutt by a passenger on the little ferry in which we crossed the Okanagan River. Perhaps the look was justified. Certainly Mutt was a quaint spectacle as he sat in the rumble seat, his goggles pushed far up on his forehead, eating cherries out of a six-quart basket.

After each cherry he would raise his muzzle, point it overside, and nonchalantly spit the pit into the green waters of the river.

12

Squirrels, Scotsmen, and Some Other Beasts

SHORTLY after I fell under the influence of my Great-uncle Frank I began to be something of a trial to my parents. Frank laid his hand upon me when I was five years old, and I have not completely evaded his shadowy grip even to this day.

He was a naturalist and collector, of the old school, who believed that everything in nature from eagles' eggs to dinosaur bones deserved house room. He also insisted that the only way to know animals was to live with them. He impressed upon me that, if it was impossible actually to live among them in the woods and fields, then the next best thing was to bring the wild folk home to live with me. I proceeded to follow his advice and on my first expedition as a budding scientist I collected, and brought home, a cow's skull and two black snakes, for which I found quarters underneath my bed.

Mother said that snakes were not fit companions for a five-year-old, but Frank—who had a good deal of authority in the family—took my side and the snakes remained with us for some weeks, until the landlord of our apartment heard about them.

Those snakes were only the first of an interminable procession of beasts, furred, feathered, and finned, which I inflicted upon my parents. It is to their eternal credit that they managed somehow to bear with most of my houseguests, nor did they attempt to discourage my bent toward practical zoology. I think Mother had some hope that I would become another Thoreau; or it may be that she simply preferred to have me declare my pets openly, rather than have me secrete them against the inevitable, and startling, moment of discovery.

There were a few such moments anyway. There was the time I kept rattlesnakes in a bookcase—but that incident passed off harmlessly enough. Then there was the time when I was six years old and was staying for a week with my paternal grandmother. One afternoon I went fishing with another lad and we caught half a dozen mud pouts, or catfish, as some people call them. I brought the fish home so that I could live with them.

Grandmother Mowat was an immensely dignified and rather terrifying old lady who did not easily tolerate the pranks of youth. Yet it was with no intention of playing a practical joke on anyone that I placed my mud pouts in the toilet bowl. I had no other choice, since there were no laundry tubs in the house, and the bathtub drain leaked so badly that you had to keep the tap running when you took a bath.

I was honestly and tearfully penitent when the mud pouts were discovered—and penitence was needed. Grandmother made the discovery herself, at a late hour when the rest of the household was fast asleep.

She forgave me, for she had a knowing heart. But I doubt that she ever fully forgave my parents.

All through the early years before we moved to Saskatoon, our rented homes and apartments housed not only us three, but a wide variety of other beasts as well. In Trenton I had a Blanding's tortoise—a rare terrestrial turtle of which I was immensely proud, and which one day distinguished itself beyond all other turtles by talking. True, it spoke but once, and then under unusual circumstances. Nevertheless, it actually did speak.

Some of my parents' friends were visiting our house, and they were kind enough to humor me and ask to see my turtle. Proudly I got it out of the box of sand where it normally lived, and released it on the dining-room table. I was chagrined when it refused to poke so much as a leg out of its shell. In exasperation I prodded it with a pencil.

Slowly it protruded its head, peered sadly up at us out of its old-woman's face, and then in the clearest, but most despondent, tones imaginable it spoke a single word.

"Yalk!" it said—as distinctly as that—and without further preamble laid an egg upon the tabletop.

I kept that jelly-bean-shaped leathery object on top of the stove for seven months, but it never hatched. I suppose my turtle must have been a virgin.

We left Trenton not long afterwards and moved to Windsor. Point Pelee National Park was only thirty miles away, and we used to drive to it on week ends so that I could do field work in natural history. One day I spied what looked like a crow's nest in a tall pine, and I climbed up to investigate. It turned out to be a black squirrel's nest containing three young squirrels.

Naturally I brought one of them home with me, carrying it inside my shirt. Without really meaning to I rather overdid Great-uncle Frank's precept, for I spent the next few days living very close to a band of several hundred fleas.

The little squirrel took readily to captivity. We called him Jitters, and Father built a cage for him that hung over the kitchen sink. It had a door that he could open and shut by himself, and he had the run of the house, and later of the neighborhood. He was an ingratiating little beast and one of his favorite diversions was boxing. He would sit on the back of a chair and box with us, using his front paws against our forefingers.

Jitters liked people, but he hated cats and he waged a bitter vendetta against them. Our own cat, whose name was Miss Stella (after our landlady of the moment), became incurably neurotic as a result of the torment inflicted on her by the squirrel, and eventually she left home forever. The cats of our neighbors suffered severely too.

It was Jitters's delight to seek out an unwary cat sunning itself beneath a tree, or under the lee of a house wall. Jitters would then quietly climb high above his victim and launch himself into space like a diving sparrow hawk. Since these leaps were often made from twenty or thirty feet up, the impact when he struck was sufficient to leave the poor cat breathless. By the time it recovered,

Jitters would have scampered to a safe vantage point from which he could taunt his enemy.

We had Jitters for over a year, and in the end it was his cat baiting that killed him. He died rather horribly. One afternoon he launched himself from halfway up the wall of our three-story apartment building and landed, not on what he had supposed was a sleeping cat, but upon a foxskin neckpiece laid to air on a concrete balustrade.

By the time we moved to Saskatoon my parents tended to take my interest in natural history for granted. Yet even they were startled one night shortly after we arrived in Saskatoon.

Mother was having a dinner party that evening for a number of local people whom we had only recently met. When dinner was ready she called to me up the back stairs, and I came down to join the party, a little dreamily, for my mind was filled with the thrill of a great discovery.

I had just begun to practice dissections, and that day I had found a dead gopher that proved to be an ideal subject for experiment. When Mother called me I had just completed my preliminary work. I had removed most of the internal organs and placed them in a saucer of formaldehyde solution. The problem of identifying all these parts was a nice one, and I was so preoccupied with it that I brought the saucer with me to the dinner table.

It was a candle-lit dinner, and no one noticed my saucer until after soup had been served. I finished my soup before anyone else and decided to employ the waiting moments by continuing with my investigations. I was so lost in them that I was not aware of the peculiar dying away of conversation on either side, until my father's voice aroused me.

"What in heaven's name have you got there, Farley?" he demanded sharply.

I answered eagerly—for I had just that instant made a momentous discovery and one that I was anxious to share.

"Dad," I cried, "you'll never guess. I've got the uterus of a gopher *and she was pregnant!*"

Hector MacCrimmon was among the guests that night, but he survived the experience to become one of our best friends. The thirty bachelor years that he had spent in Canada since leaving Caithness in northern Scotland had not altered either his accent or his Presbyterian sense of rectitude. For twenty years his home had been a room in one of Saskatoon's hotels, and if ever a man was immovably settled into a habitual pattern of life, it was surely Hector.

Nevertheless, when we moved our caravan out to the Saskatoon Country Club for the summer months, we pressed Hector to join us for a bucolic week end.

He would have refused the invitation outright if he could have done so gracefully, for he had no love of the out-of-doors. His hotel life may have been dull and confining, but it was comfortable, and Hector was eminently a comfortable sort of man. He evaded the issue of the country week end with skill and perseverance, but in the end we were too much for him, and in mid-August he found himself committed to a three-day visit. It was in a mood of Christian resignation that he eventually arrived, for he put little faith in my father's glowing assurances that we lived in the very lap of luxury.

Squirrels, Scotsmen, and Some Other Beasts

Our camp was on the riverbank, in a dense stand of poplar. The caravan stood in a little clearing, with the open-air fireplace before it and farther back toward the trees an umbrella tent, which was the private place where I lived and slept. My parents had decided that Hector should have my unoccupied bunk in the caravan, but when Hector heard of this arrangement he was horrified.

"I'll nae do it!" he cried vehemently. "Wud ye have me sleep between a mon and his lawful spouse? Foosh and for shame! Come, Angus, sin ye have no place for me to lay my haid, I'll be away back to Saskatoon for the night."

I don't know how much of that outburst was really due to his Presbyterian scruples, and how much of it was due to a last-minute, but canny, attempt to escape from country living. But if it was escape he had in mind, he was doomed to failure.

"Nonsense," Father replied heartily. "You can sleep on the spare cot in Farley's tent. That should be decent enough even for an old Puritan like you, but"—and here my father's voice betrayed a trace of hesitation—"it may not be quite as peaceful there as in the caravan."

Hector knew that he was beaten, but he would have the last word. "Peaceful!" he said bleakly. "Ther'll be little peace for me until I'm hame."

It was a prophetic statement.

After supper my elders remained around the fire, drinking hot toddy and swatting at mosquitoes. I retired directly to my tent, for I had chores to do.

During that summer I had made a strenuous effort to obey the injunctions of Great-uncle Frank, and as a result the tent had become far more than a bedroom. It had become a place where I could live in really close contact with nature, for I shared the tenancy with a dozen chipmunks, a partially tamed long-eared owl, three bushy-tailed wood gophers, a least weasel, and a baker's dozen of garter snakes. Each species had its own quarters. The snakes lived in a cardboard carton under my bed; the weasel in a gallon-size tin can; the chipmunks in an orange crate faced with fly screening; the wood gophers in a wooden tub; while the owl was free to range at the end of a long piece of twine tied to the tent pole. The makeshift cages were not all they might have been, and whenever I went into the tent I could usually count on finding some of my comrades on the loose. However, on this particular evening Father had drawn me aside after dinner to warn me sternly that there must be no escapes that night.

Having made everything secure, I went to bed. I awakened briefly at Hector's belated arrival in the tent some hours later. He undressed in darkness, fearing perhaps that it would be indecent to do so by the light of the electric torch with which he was provided.

A number of mosquitoes had followed him into the tent, and although they did not bother me (for I buried my head under my sheet), they seemed to annoy Hector. He muttered and thrashed about for a long time.

Sometime well after midnight I was awakened again by the detonation of thunder overhead. Coincidental with the earth-shaking crash there was a disturbance at the tent door, and Mutt pushed his way inside. He was inordinately frightened of thunderstorms, and when this one burst, he abandoned his usual sleeping quarters under the caravan and fled to me for solace and protection.

I could see Hector, outlined against the flailing canvas by the flicker of the lightning, sitting up in his bed and thrusting one long leg, like a Masai spear, at something between the two cots.

"Whoosh!" he cried sharply. "What was that?"

"It's nothing, Mr. MacCrimmon," I replied. "Only Mutt coming in to get out of the rain."

"Mutt be dommed!" Hector yelled. "It's the deil himself!"

At that moment Mutt, who had crawled under my cot, gave a convulsive leap that almost overturned the bed. Immediately there was a scampering across my blankets that told me my chipmunks were no longer in their little home. Hector was now lashing about with arms and legs and making such violent contact with the walls of the tent that I was afraid the whole thing would collapse. "It's all right; it's only chipmunks!" I called in an attempt to soothe him.

He did not waste his breath in a reply. He had found his flashlight, and suddenly its yellow beam flooded the tent. I saw at once that I had been wrong. It had been neither Mutt nor the chipmunks that had been bothering him. It was my owl, which was now crouching in a belligerent attitude on Hector's pillow, gripping the still-wriggling body of a wood gopher in its talons. There was a look in the owl's eye that boded no good for anyone who tried to interfere with it.

Hector had no intention of interfering. With one amazingly

agile motion he reached the other end of his bed. He huddled there for a moment as if uncertain what to do next, and then he made up his mind and swung both feet down to the tent floor.

The floor was of canvas, but it was old and no longer water-proof. Sufficient rain water had already seeped through to dissolve the bottom of the cardboard snake box. The snakes were probably as upset as any of us, and when Hector stepped on one of them, the poor beast coiled convulsively around his ankle.

Hector's vocal response to this new stimulus was so impressive that it wakened my parents in the caravan. Through the drumming of the rain, and the rumble of the thunder, I could hear my father's voice crying with some asperity:

"Wake up! Wake u-u-u-u-up, Hecto-r-r-r-r! You're having a nightmare!"

And that, as Hector admitted to a mutual friend in the Albert Hotel some weeks later, "was no so verra far from the truth, if ye ken what I mean!"

That long-eared owl was the first of my owls. It was followed by many more—but of them all, by far the most memorable were the two great horned owls which joined our family in the following year.

The natural-science teacher at my school was a keen wildlife photographer and it was his ambition to take a series of pictures of a great horned owl. He enlisted my aid to discover a nest. This was a mission in the following spring. I began my search, in company with Bruce Billings, a youngster of my own age and inclinations.

Every week end Bruce and I would pack our haversacks and

tramp the poplar bluffs looking for owls. At night we would build a lean-to shelter, or "wickiup," out of branches. Then we would make our supper fire and cook a meal of bacon and eggs and tea. As darkness came down we would lie on the new-greening grass and listen to the prairie sing. From far off would come the yelping of a coyote, answered and echoed by others, and dying away at last into a distance beyond hearing. From the sloughs the frogs would babble, and the shrill piping of night-migrating sandpipers would come on the dark wind. Sometimes we were stirred by the reverberating cry of sandhill cranes so high above us that when they crossed the moon's face, they were no more than midges.

But our ears were not really tuned to these voices. We were listening for the gruff "hoo-hoo-hoo" of horned owls, and when at last one of them would call, we would lay sticks upon the ground, pointing toward the sound.

With the first pallid dawn we would be awake, damp with the dew, and eager for the warmth of the breakfast fire. Later we would take our bearings from the direction the sticks pointed and, with Mutt romping ahead as an advance guard, would begin searching every poplar bluff along the indicated line of march.

It was always a long search, but never tedious. Every bluff had its occupants and if they were not the ones we sought, they were fascinating in themselves. Along the edges of the copses, wood gophers would chuckle fearlessly at us, for they seem to have a liking for man, and do not flee him as do their saffron-colored brothers of the open plains. Within each bluff itself there would usually be at least one large nest high in the poplars. Often it was a crow's home, and the raucous scolding of the owners would follow us for miles. Sometimes it was the immense, roofed nest of a pair of magpies. Sometimes it was an old crow's nest now occupied by long-eared owls whose sly, cat faces would peer at us nervously as we walked by. Sometimes the nest would belong to a pigeon hawk, the trimmest of the little falcons; or to a pair of the great-winged hawks, Swainson's or redtails.

And between the bluffs, in the short new grass, meadowlarks and vesper sparrows would burst from underfoot, their nests hidden from us until Mutt's snuffling nose found them out. Mutt never disturbed birds' nests. He only found them for us and then stood by while we poked and peered, and occasionally took one of the eggs.

The moment when at last we halted beneath the untidy bulk of a large nest in a high poplar and, staring upward, could identify the home of the greatest of the owls was an intensely thrilling one. It was an emotion to be matched only by the excitement of climbing the tree, with eyes cautiously averted, and yet with many a furtive glance at the huge bird above. Only once was I ever actually struck by a defending owl, and then it was a glancing blow that probably resulted from a miscalculation on the owl's part. But the wind-rushing dive of a bird with a five-foot wingspread, as it swerved to miss my head by a hand's breadth, was as thrilling to a boy as ever the charge of an attacking lion was to a grown man.

Once we had found a nest and had assured ourselves that it was occupied, we would report the news to our teacher friend, and in the days that followed we would help him build his blind. These

Squirrels, Scotsmen, and Some Other Beasts

blinds were rickety affairs of branches and canvas, tied and nailed in the tree-tops adjacent to the nest. The owls seldom took kindly to the arrival of neighbors and on one occasion an owl attacked the face of a newly built blind, ripping the tough canvas to shreds with its inch-long talons. But eventually the blind would become no more than another part of the landscape and the birds would ignore it, and its occupants. For long, hot hours, I used to sit hidden from the owls, and watch their lives. I seldom used the camera that I carried, for I was too fascinated by the birds themselves. At first they seemed no more than brute beasts, bloodied with the game they brought back, yellow-eyed and savage to behold. But in time I began to see them differently—as living things whose appetites, and fears, and perhaps pleasures too were not so very different from my own.

I grew more and more enamored of them.

When we were preparing to leave the last of the three nests we had photographed that spring, I decided that I was not yet ready to sever my acquaintance with these interesting birds and so I carried one of the young ones home with me in my haversack.

The owlet was still flightless, and still possessed of much of his fledgling down. Nevertheless, he had presence, and we decided that he should be named Wol, after Christopher Robin's sage but bumbling old friend.

Later that summer I came by yet another young horned owl. I found him held prisoner in an oil barrel where he had been placed by a bevy of youths who were intent on destroying him by inches. Bedraggled, filthy, and exhausted, he was a pitiful sight when I first beheld him. I parted with a hunting knife that was a prized possession, and found myself the owner of a second owl.

We named this one Weeps, for he never got over his oil-barrel experiences, and he never stopped keening as long as we knew him.

He and Wol were as different in character as two individuals could be. Wol was self-assured, domineering, and certain of his place in the sun. Weeps was timorous and retiring, and convinced that fate was his enemy. They differed in appearance, too, for Wol was of the arctic subspecies and his adult plumage was almost pure white, touched only lightly with black markings. Weeps, on the other hand, was a drab and sooty brown and his feathers always appeared shabby and frayed at the ends.

These two were among the most fascinating animals that I have ever known. They gave me a great deal of pleasure—but they made Mutt's life a hell on earth.

13

Owls Underfoot

When the owls first joined our family they were less than six weeks old, but already giving promise that their ultimate size would be impressive. My parents, who had never seen a full-grown horned owl, had no real idea as to just *how* impressive they could be, and I preserved a discreet silence on the subject. Nevertheless, Mother vetoed my plan for keeping the two newest, and youngest, members of the family in my bedroom, even though I pointed out to her that the birds might get lost, and in any case they would be in considerable danger from cats and dogs if they were kept outside.

Mother looked speculatively at the talons which the unhappy fledglings were flexing—talons already three quarters of an inch in length—and gave it as her considered opinion that the cats and dogs would have a thin time of it in a mix-up with the owls. As to their getting lost—my mother was always an optimist.

Eventually my father solved the housing problem by helping me build a large chicken-wire enclosure in the back yard. This enclosure was used only a few months, for it soon became superfluous.

The Dog Who Wouldn't Be

In the first place, the owls showed no disposition to stray from their new home. Each day I would take them out for a romp on the lawn and, far from attempting to return to their wild haunts, they displayed an overwhelming anxiety to avoid the uncertainties of freedom. Once or twice I accidentally left them alone in the yard and they, concluding that they had been abandoned, staged a determined retreat into the house itself. Screen doors were no barrier to them, for the copper mesh melted under the raking impact of their talons as if it had been tissue paper. Both owls would then come bursting through the shattered screen into the kitchen, breathing hard, and looking apprehensively over their shoulders at the wide outer world where their unwanted freedom lay.

Consequently the back-yard cage became not so much a means of keeping the owls with us, as a means of keeping them from being too closely with us.

The two fledglings were utterly unlike in character. Wol, the dominant member of the pair, was a calmly arrogant extrovert who knew that he was the world's equal. Weeps, on the other hand, was a nervous, inconsequential bird of an unsettled disposition; and plagued by nebulous fears. Weeps was a true neurotic, and though his brother learned to be housebroken in a matter of a few weeks, Weeps never could be trusted on the furniture and rugs.

When they were three months old, and nearly full grown (although tufts of baby down still adhered to their feathers), Wol confirmed Mother's first impression as to his ability to defend himself. At three months of age he stood almost two feet high. His wingspread was in the neighborhood of four feet. His talons were an inch in length and needle sharp, and, combined with his hooked beak, they gave him a formidable armament.

One summer night he was in a huff as the result of a disagreement he had had with Mutt. When darkness fell he refused to come down from a high perch in a poplar tree in order to go to bed in the safe refuge of the cage. Since there was nothing we could do to persuade him, we finally left him in his tree and went to bed ourselves.

Knowing something of the ferocity of the night-stalking cats of Saskatoon, I was uneasy for him and I slept lightly, with one ear cocked. It was just breaking dawn when I heard the sound of a muffled flurry in the back yard. I leaped from my bed, grabbed my rifle, and rushed out of the front door.

To my horror there was no sign of Wol. The poplar trees were empty. Suspecting the worst, I raced around the corner of the house, my bare feet slipping in the dew-wet grass.

Wol was sitting quietly on the back steps, his body hunched up in an attitude of somnolent comfort. The scene could hardly have been more peaceful.

It was not until I came close, and had begun to remonstrate with him the chances he had taken, that I saw the cat.

Wol was sitting on it. His feathers were fluffed out in the manner of sleeping birds so that only the cat's head and tail were visible. Nevertheless, I saw enough to realize that the cat was beyond mortal aid.

The Dog Who Wouldn't Be

Wol protested when I lifted him clear of his victim. I think he had been enjoying the warmth of his footrest, for the cat had been dead only a few moments. I took it quickly to the foot of the garden and buried it circumspectly, for I recognized it as the big ginger tom from two doors down the street. It had long been the terror of birds and dogs and fellow cats throughout our neighborhood. Its owner was a big man with a loud and raucous voice who did not like small boys.

The ginger tom was the first, but not the last, feline to fall into error about Wol. In time the secret cemetery at the bottom of the garden became crowded with the remains of cats who had assumed that Wol was just another kind of chicken and therefore easy meat.

Nor were dogs much more of a problem to the owls. Rather grudgingly, for he was jealous of them, Mutt undertook to protect them from others of his own race. Several times he saved Weeps from a mauling, but Wol did not really need his protection. One evening a German shepherd—a cocksure bully if ever there was one—who lived not far from our house caught Wol on the ground and went for him with murder in his eye. It was a surprisingly one-sided battle. Wol lost a handful of feathers, but the dog went under the care of a veterinary, and for weeks afterwards he would cross the street to avoid passing too close to our house—and to Wol.

Despite his formidable fighting abilities, Wol was seldom the aggressor. Those other beasts which, like man, have developed the unnatural blood lusts that go with civilization would have found Wol's restraint rather baffling, for he used his powerful weapons only to protect himself, or to fill his belly, and never simply for the joy of killing. There was no moral or ethical philosophy behind his restraint—there was only the indisputable fact that killing, for its own sake, gave him no pleasure. Although perhaps, if he and his descendants had lived long enough in human company, he might have become as sanguinary and as cruel as we conceive all other carnivores—except ourselves—to be.

Feeding the owls was not much of a problem. Weeps ate anything that was set before him, on the theory—apparently— that each meal was his last. The future always looked black to him—such was his sad nature. Wol, on the other hand, was more demanding. Hard-boiled eggs, hamburger, cold roast beef, and fig cookies were his chosen articles of diet. Occasionally he would deign to tear apart a gopher that one of the neighborhood boys had snared on the prairie beyond the city; but on the whole he did not relish wild game—with one notable exception.

It has been said by scientists, who should know better, that the skunk has no natural enemies. It is this sort of smug generalization that gives scientists a bad name. Skunks *have* one enemy in nature—a voracious and implacable enemy—the great horned owl.

There can be few animal feuds as relentless as the one which has raged between horned owls and skunks for uncounted aeons. I have no idea how it originally started, but I know quite a lot about the tenacity with which it is still pursued.

The faintest whiff of skunk on a belated evening breeze would transform the usually calm and benign Wol into a winged fury.

The Dog Who Wouldn't Be

Unfortunately our house stood on the banks of the Saskatchewan River, and there was a belt of underbrush along the shore which provided an ideal highway for wandering skunks. Occasionally one of them would forgo the riverbank and do his arrogant promenading on the sidewalk in front of our house.

The first time this happened was in the late summer of Wol's first year. The skunk, cocksure and smug as are all the members of his species, came down the sidewalk just as dusk was falling. Some children who were playing under the poplar trees fled the approaching outcast, as did an elderly woman who was airing her Pekinese. Swollen with his own foolish pride, the skunk strutted on until he came beneath the overhanging branches in front of the Mowat home.

Our windows were open and we were just finishing a late dinner. There was not much breeze, and by the time the first acrid warning came wafting into the dining room, Wol himself was ready to make his entrance. He came through the open window in a shallow dive and fetched up on the floor, depositing the still-quivering skunk beside my chair.

"Hoo-hoohoohoo-HOO," he said proudly. Which, translated, probably meant "Mind if I join you? I've brought my own lunch."

Owls are not widely renowned for their sense of humor, and Wol may have been an exception, but he, at least, possessed an almost satanic fondness for practical jokes, of which poor Mutt was usually the victim. He would steal Mutt's bones and cache them in the crotch of a tree trunk just far enough above the ground to be beyond Mutt's reach. He would join Mutt at dinner sometimes, and by dint of sheer bluff, force the hungry and unhappy dog away from the dish, and keep him away until finally the game palled. Wol never actually *ate* Mutt's food. That would have been beneath him.

His favorite joke, though, was the tail squeeze.

During the searing heat of the summer afternoons Mutt would try to snooze the blistering hours away in a little hollow which he had excavated beneath the hedge on our front lawn. However, before withdrawing to this sanctuary he would make a careful cast about the grounds until he had located Wol, and had assured himself that the owl was either asleep or at least deep in meditation. Only then would Mutt retire to his repose, and dare to close his eyes.

Despite a hundred bitter demonstrations of the truth, Mutt never understood that Wol seldom slept. Sometimes the owl's great yellow orbs would indeed be hooded, but even then—though he might appear to be as insensible as a graven bird—he retained a delicate awareness of all that was happening around him. His eyesight was so phenomenally acute as to completely discredit the old canard that owls are blind in daylight. Often I have seen him start from what appeared to be a profound trance, if not slumber, and, half turning his head, stare full into the blaze of the noonday sky while crouching down upon his roost in an attitude of taut belligerence. Following the direction of his gaze with my unaided eyes, I could seldom find anything threatening in the white sky; but when I brought my binoculars into play they would invariably reveal a soaring hawk or eagle so high above us that even through the glasses it seemed to be no bigger than a mote of dust.

In any event, Mutt's suspicious reconnoitering before he gave himself up to sleep was usually ineffective and, worse than that, it served to alert Wol to the fact that his quarry would soon be vulnerable.

Wol was a bird of immense patience. He would sometimes wait half an hour after Mutt had slunk away to rest before he began his stalk. He always stalked Mutt on foot, as if disdaining the advantage given him by his powers of flight.

Infinitely slowly, and with the grave solemnity of a mourner at a funeral, he would inch his way across the lawn. If Mutt stirred in his sleep, Wol would freeze and remain motionless for long minutes—his gaze fixed and unblinking on his ultimate objective—Mutt's long and silken tail.

Sometimes it took him an hour to reach his goal. But at last he would arrive within range and then, with ponderous deliberation, he would raise one foot and poise it—as if to fully savor the delicious moment—directly over Mutt's proud plume. Then, suddenly, the outspread talons would drop, and clutch. ...

Invariably Mutt woke screaming. Leaping to his feet, he would spin around, intent on punishing his tormentor—and would find him not. From the branch of a poplar tree well above his head would come a sonorous and insulting "Hoo-HOO-hoo-hoo," which, I suspect, is about as close to laughter as an owl can come.

It seemed to be inevitable that any animal which we took into our family would soon cease to consider itself anything less than human; and it was so with Wol. Very early in life he took note of the fact that we others could not, or would not, fly, and he thereupon accepted a terrestrial way of life for which he was but poorly adapted.

When I visited the little corner store, some three blocks from home, Wol would usually accompany me, and he would walk. Strangers who did not know him (and there were few such in Saskatoon) were apt to be severely startled when they encountered him during one of these promenades, for he walked with a lumbering, rolling gait that smacked of a lifetime of alcoholism. Furthermore, he gave ground to no man. If a pedestrian bound upstream happened upon Wol going downstream, the pedestrian either moved aside or there was a collision. These collisions were not to be taken lightly. I recall all too vividly an occasion when a new postman, rapt in the perusal of the unfamiliar addresses on a bundle of letters, walked full into Wol one summer morning. The man was so completely preoccupied with his own problems that he did not even bother to glance down to ascertain the nature of the obstruction in his path, but blindly tried to kick it to one side. This, to Wol, was tantamount to deliberate assault. IIe rose on his dignity—which was immense—uttered a piercing hiss, and banged the offending human on the shins with his mighty wings. (Nor was this a gentle form of retaliation.) There was a sharp crack. The postman yelped in sudden pain, peered down at his feet, yelled even louder (this time on a high, keening note), and fled the neighborhood. It was left for me to collect the scattered letters and pursue him with what I hoped were appropriate apologies.

The Dog Who Wouldn't Be

When school began again that fall I experienced some difficulty with the owls, but in particular with Wol. My school was on the opposite side of the river, a good three miles from home, and I reached it by bicycling over the Twenty-fifth Street bridge. When I began going to classes in September the owls were indignant, for they, who had been my constant companions all that summer, were now left alone. They did not readily accept this new state of affairs and, during the first week of the term, I was late on three successive days as a result of having to conduct my tenacious pair of followers back home.

On the fourth morning I grew desperate and tried locking them in the big outdoor pen—which they had long since ceased to use. Wol was infuriated by this treatment and he tore into the chicken-wire barrier with angry talons. I sneaked hurriedly away, but before I was halfway across the bridge a startled shout from a pedestrian, and the scream of brakes from a passing car, alerted me to some unusual happenstance. I had barely time to apply my own brakes when there was a wild rush of air, a deep-throated and victorious "Hoo-HOO!" and two sets of talons settled themselves securely on my shoulder. Wol was breathless from the unaccustomed business of flying, but he was triumphant.

It was by then too late to take him home again, so I went resignedly on my way to school. I left him in the yard, perched on the handlebars of my bicycle, and insecurely tied with binder twine.

My third class that morning happened to be French. The teacher was a desiccated female whose spiritual home may have been Paris, but who had never actually been farther east than

Owls Underfoot

Winnipeg. She was affected, humorless, and a tyrant. None of us liked her. Yet I actually felt sorry for her when, in the midst of the declination of an irregular verb, Wol whumped moodily in through the second-story window and slid to an unsatisfactory halt upon the top of her hardwood desk. The exclamation with which she greeted him was given in very old Anglo-Saxon, without even a hint of a French accent.

I had an interview with the principal after this incident, but he was a reasonable man and the upshot was that I escaped corporal punishment on the understanding that my owl would stay at home in future.

I achieved this end, but only at the cost of giving the owls the free run of our house. Some ten minutes before I was due to leave for school I would invite Weeps and Wol into the kitchen, where they were allowed to finish off the bacon scraps left from our breakfast. Apparently Wol accepted this as a sufficient bribe, for he made no further attempt to follow me to school; and Weeps, who always accepted Wol's lead, gave me no more trouble either. Mother, on the other hand, was not best pleased by these arrangements.

Although the majority of the human residents of Saskatoon knew about, and were inured to, our owls, there were at least two occasions when Wol and Weeps were the unwitting cause of some alarm and despondency to members of the human species. One of these took place in a prairie hamlet to the north of Saskatoon. It was in August, and my parents had decided that we should spend a week end at Emma Lake, a resort area far to the north. We loaded our camping gear aboard Eardlie and the six of us—Mother, Father, myself, Mutt, and the two owls—set out.

Having ridden in the car on several previous occasions, the owls had developed a preference in the matter of seating arrangements. Their chosen roost was the back of the rumble seat, where they were exposed to the full force of the slip stream. They loved it, for it offered them the same exhilarating thrill that all small boys experience when they thrust a hand out of a car window and let the wind act on it as it does upon the wing of an aircraft. My owls exploited this adventure to the limit. As soon as the car was in motion they would extended their great pinions as if in flight. If they then slanted the leading edges downward, the rush of air would force them into a squatting position. But when they tipped the leading edges upward, they would be lifted clean off the seat, and only the grip of their talons would keep them from soaring aloft like kites.

There was not sufficient room to allow both of them to bob up and down together, so they learned to alternate. While one was going down, the other would be coming up, in rhythmic frequency. Intoxicated by the rush of air, they would often break into song, and my father, caught up in the spirit of the thing, would punctuate their excited hootings with blasts on Eardlie's horn.

Mutt also rode in the rumble seat, his eyes protected from the inevitable prairie dust by his motorcycle goggles. Thus the complete picture of Eardlie on the highways included a vignette of Mutt sitting stolidly between two active owls, and staring straight ahead through his outsize goggles with a kind of dour resignation.

At the time I never considered the effect that this apparition must have had upon the drivers of farm wagons whom we passed; and upon the drivers of other cars who passed us. But I have since had some penitential thoughts about the matter.

On the day we started north the sky was threatening, and we had only gone fifty or sixty miles when a thin drizzle began to beat upon the windscreen. The drizzle quickly thickened, and we halted to erect the canvas hood over the front seat. By the time we had finished, the rain had become a downpour, and when we drove off again, the rumble seat and its occupants were receiving a mighty scourging from the storm. Mutt wisely hunched himself down into the seat well where he was less exposed to the fury of wind and water, but the owls refused to abandon their exposed perch. They even seemed to be enjoying the pelting rain, although their feathers were soon plastered to their bodies, and their great wings hung sodden and drooping.

Eardlie was the one who really suffered from the deluge, and he began to cough and sputter alarmingly just as we entered one of those two-elevator, one-store, one-garage villages which sprout like toadstools on the western plains. The garage in this particular village was a scrofulous frame shanty with a single antiquated gasoline pump in front of it. A black doorway gaped in the façade and, presuming that this led to the workshop, my father wheeled Eardlie through the thickening gumbo of the street and into the interior of the building.

The garage was dark and gloomy. A single meager light bulb glowed dismally, high up among the rafters, and by its wan and pallid rays we could barely distinguish the clutter of old tractor parts and rusted scrap that almost filled the place. The proprietor was not immediately in evidence and we were about to dismount and go searching for him when my eye was caught by movement near Eardlie's right rear fender.

A man was crouching in the shadows there, apparently brooding over an old inner tube. He had a tire iron in his hand and he seemed quite oblivious to our presence.

We waited with what patience we could muster until he finished communing with the tube and then, very slowly, he began to straighten his back and stand up to our level.

His face came into view about three feet away from the rumble seat. I can see that face as clearly now as I saw it then. It was pallid, deeply lined, and petulant, and smeared with grease that had stiffened a week-old beard. It was wearing a look of querulous animosity, but this began to change as the eyes focused themselves on the car and its passengers. The pallidity of the face was accentuated in a startling manner. The jaws began to move as they might in a ruminant—though they were chewing on nothing more substantial than empty air.

It was then that Wol chose to shake himself. He spread his wings to their full extent, gave a little leap, and sprayed water far and wide. The shake transformed him, increasing his apparent size about threefold as his wet feathers came unstuck. The transition was startling enough; but when he concluded the performance by loudly clacking his great beak, by flipping the membranes sickeningly over his yellow eyes, and by giving throaty voice to his relief—the effect was devastating.

The garageman's face indicated that at least *he* found it so. The tempo of his jaw speeded up and his face registered a look of fearful, and then desperate, incomprehension.

Perhaps Mutt was as curious as were the rest of us, for at this moment he chose to thrust his goggled head over the edge of the car for a closer look, peering in his short-sighted manner into the garageman's face.

The man had had enough. He moaned low in his throat, threw the tire iron recklessly over his shoulder, but did not stay to hear the crash of broken glass as the sole window shattered. He was gone by then, running down the muddy street, his lank arms held high above his head and the rain beating into his face.

"Oh, Jesu!" he was crying. "Oh, Sweet Jesu! I never *done* it, that I'll *swear!*"

Mother was shocked. She felt that this was a foolish and sacrilegious thing to say. But how could she know? I have often speculated since on the nature of that man's hidden crime, for there must have been small enough scope for sin in that desolate and meager little village.

More than a year elapsed, and Wol had become a full-fledged member of the family, before he struck once more at human sanity. He had, by this time, become a house owl, making almost as much use of the house as we did ourselves. It was useless to try to deny him house privileges, for he had learned that when he came and banged on the window panes with his horny beak, we would hasten to admit him before the glass gave way. During the warm seasons we resigned ourselves to leaving one of the living-room windows permanently open, and by this portal he would come and go as the mood was on him.

In the summer of Wol's second year, Saskatoon was enriched by the arrival of a young curate who had just graduated from a divinity school in the east. The curate was of an earnest persuasion and he made it his first duty to pay a call on every one of the members of our parish (to which he was attached). It was a warm and balmy summer afternoon when he reached our house.

He rang our doorbell, and Mother was pleased to welcome him, for he was a well-favored youth. He had the high-domed forehead that is so often the mark of the stage cleric, but the hair above it was black and curly. Mother invited him into the living room for a chat and a cup of tea.

The young man made himself discreetly comfortable on our chesterfield, a massive and antique piece of furniture which was so placed that it faced the fireplace, with its back to the open window some six feet behind it. Balancing a cup gracefully in his hand, the young divine engaged Mother in conversation, the burden of which was concerned with my own lamentable absence from Sunday School.

Wol had been spending that afternoon ant bathing. This was a peculiar pastime in which he sometimes engaged, and which consisted of tearing an anthill apart and then fluffing the mixture of dust and angry ants through his feathers. He appeared to find the sensation gratifying, although its purpose seemed inscrutable to us. At any rate, he finished his bath about 4 P.M. and, feeling in an amiable mood, decided to come into the house and tell Mother about it.

Owls Underfoot

To this day my mother swears she did not see him in sufficient time to warn her visitor. I believe that she saw him well enough, but was just too petrified to open her mouth.

Now Wol, in his maturity, had become a sentimental bird, possessed of the habit of leaping lightly to one's shoulder, there to balance himself while he tenderly nibbled the nearest human ear with his great beak, breathing harshly but affectionately into the face of his companion the while. Everyone who was acquainted with Wol knew of this habit, and some deplored it, for Wol was a carnivore and as a result he had the most atrocious breath.

The flight of an owl is noiseless; there is no warning rustle of pinions. Wol's arrival on the windowsill was as silent as the arrival of a puff of thistledown. He paused a moment in the opening and then, spying a pair of tempting shoulders on the chesterfield, launched himself across the narrow intervening space.

The object of his attentions shot straightway into the air and began leaping ecstatically about the room. It was an ill-considered action on his part, for Wol lost his balance and, with a purely involuntary reflex action, tightened up his talons.

The curate now demonstrated that he was both an athletic and a vocal youth. He howled, and his bouncing became wilder. Wol, clinging for dear life now, and deeply disturbed by his reception, tightened up his grip once more and then—and it could have happened only as a result of his surprise and indignation—he forgot for the first and last time in his mature life that he was house-broken....

I do not recall any single catastrophe among the many which

beset my family through the years that caused us quite as much embarrassment as this one did. Mother, who was a pillar of the church, suffered more than the rest of us, but my father and I were not exempt. I can but hope that the church officials noticed how well filled the Mowat collection envelopes were on succeeding Sundays. I hope too that the elders of the church had the common decency to reimburse their new curate for dry-cleaning expenses incurred, let us say, in the line of duty.

The stories of my family and Wol and Weeps that I have so far related are only highlights of a relationship which, on the whole, was a warm and rewarding one. Even my mother, who had less reason than any of us for such an attitude, was fond of Wol and she forgave him almost everything during the three years he was with us. Though our owls were often underfoot, both actually and figuratively, we would not willingly have eschewed the chance to live with them.

But as it must be with the lives of most wild things which have been taken from the wilderness, the final fate of the two owls was a tragic one. When we left the west permanently in 1935, it proved impossible to take them with us; and so we reluctantly made arrangements with an acquaintance who owned a farm some two hundred miles from Saskatoon to care for our old friends. It was, of course, out of the question to turn them loose, for they would have been as helpless in the outer world as newborn owlets.

For almost a year we had good reports of both our birds; but then poor ineffectual Weeps somehow managed to strangle himself in the wire netting of his cage. Only a few weeks later Wol tore the mesh apart and vanished.

I wish that he had vanished permanently.

Before we left the west I tagged both owls with aluminum bands supplied by the U. S. Biological Survey. One day I received a letter from the survey informing me that a great horned owl, banded by me in Saskatoon in the spring of the year 1935, had been shot and killed in that same city in April of 1939.

The address of the man who killed the owl, and who returned the band to Washington, was given. It was the address of the house where we had once lived with Wol and Weeps.

So in the end Wol went back to that home which he had known so well. It took him almost three years to find his way, yet he succeeded. I can guess at his thoughts as he landed in the familiar old poplars and then dropped contentedly down to light upon the windowsill, and to rap imperatively upon the glass with his great beak. . . .

I hope that death was mercifully quick.

14

A Mess of Skunks

ALMOST every dog eventually runs foul of a skunk. Most dogs learn something from the experience. The wiser ones may conclude that it is common sense to defer to skunks in future, and even those tykes that habitually pursue danger tend to be more circumspect after their first encounter.

Mutt was no fool. Neither was he feckless. And this makes it even more difficult to explain his inability to grasp the fact that mixing it with skunks was unrewarding. The only beast I know of that makes a practice of attacking skunks is the great horned owl, but it has almost no sense of smell, it does not normally live in houses, and furthermore it eats the skunks it kills. Mutt, on the other hand, could smell very well, he habitually lived in houses with other and more sensitive beings, and he did not eat raw meat.

I can find no rational explanation for his foolhardy attitude toward skunks. The fact remains that there was hardly a time after he had passed his second birthday when he was not accompanied by that familiar odor—sometimes of great intensity, sometimes no more than a faint, but unmistakable, miasma in the air.

It is noteworthy that his first encounter was delayed until he had entered his third year.

It happened in July. In order to escape from the savage heat of the prairie summer, we had hauled the caravan north into the forested part of Saskatchewan, to a small resort on Lotus Lake. Mother's association with the Church of England in Saskatoon had gained us the privilege of being permitted to park our caravan on an isolated beach that belonged to the church and that was normally reserved for members of the cloth and their immediate families.

It was a most pleasant site. The caravan was close to the water's edge, on a small and private cove. There was a dock, equipped with a diving board, for our personal use. Privacy was the watchword of the place and we took advantage of it to swim without benefit of bathing suits. We were circumspect about this, for we had no wish to shock our hosts—but we were equally determined not to wear clothing in the water, unless driven to it.

We were soon driven to it. There were many young people at the beach: young divines, and young daughters of elderly divines. They were all, apparently, addicted to moonlight canoe expeditions, and our secluded cove seemed to draw them irresistibly. A canoe at night can be a stealthy thing, and much of the pleasure of our nocturnal bathing was spoiled by the irritating necessity of keeping a careful watch.

My parents felt this irritation more than did Mutt or I. Mutt had nothing to hide in any case, and I had almost as little to worry about, for I was then only twelve years old. My parents began to forgo the pleasures of the unclothed evening swim, but Mutt and I were more resolute.

Mutt was a fine swimmer, and he greatly enjoyed diving. He actually preferred to go in off the board, and it was a remarkable thing to see him bouncing slowly up and down at the end of the plank, gaining momentum for his leap.

One evening he and I left the caravan, with Mutt well in the lead. By the time I reached the shore, Mutt was halfway out the plank, and it was then too late for me to do anything but watch.

The board was already occupied. A skunk was lying at the tip of it, dreamily staring down into the moonlit waters at the schools of plump little rock bass that flickered back and forth. Innocent as he then was, Mutt nevertheless showed incredible obtuseness—the first intimation of this curious weakness that was to become so painfully familiar to us in the future. He made no effort to investigate the skunk. He simply lowered his head, flung his ears back out of his eyes, and charged.

The skunk's defensive blast caught Mutt from a range of not more than three feet, and deflected him to one side so that he ran off into space with considerable momentum and hit the water a good distance from the dock. I think that he must have actually gone right over the canoe, for when he surfaced—screaming with pain and outrage and lashing the water blindly—it was the seaward side of the canoe that his paws encountered.

I had not been aware of the canoe until then, but neither I nor any other resident of that section of the beach was left long in ignorance of its proximity. Mutt's efforts to scramble aboard completed the discomfiture of a young couple who had already reaped the wind. The man, who was a clergyman-to-be, showed a nobility of soul commensurate with his vocation. But the young lady was the daughter of a vicar—and she ran true to type. Her language was not churchly and, although I had spent much time among the tough boys who lived on the wrong side of the tracks in Saskatoon, I was impressed by this girl's virtuosity.

Our annoyance with Mutt was tempered by a degree of gratitude, for during the remainder of our stay at Lotus Lake we were untroubled by young love under the moon. Our little bay had acquired a hard name locally.

We had had our period of grace; for after this first encounter, Mutt and skunks became almost inseparable. There was a brief surcease for us during the heart of winter, but with the first spring days and the emergence of the skunks from semihibernation, we took up our cross once more.

It seemed to make no difference where we might be, in the geographical sense. On one occasion we welcomed spring in an area where no skunk had been reported for thirty years. There were skunks that spring; so many of them that the locals marveled, and spoke in hushed voices of a visitation.

Mutt's popularity was endangered by this affinity for skunks and there were people who may have wished in their hearts that Mutt had never been. Foremost among them must have been the undertaker's assistant in Happy Home Cemetery on a June day in 1939.

Happy Home lies in the heart of metropolitan Toronto and is

isolated from the nearest wilderness by miles of asphalt desert. Yet it is very green and, in the spring at least, lovely with bird song. It is well named, for with its trees and brooks it is an oasis in the gray desolation of the city. Almost anyone could be happy there. Certainly Mutt and I found it a happy place, for it was our retreat during the blighted year we lived in Toronto. We spent many hours in Happy Home, looking for birds or simply meandering among the willow trees. We harbored the dream that some day we should encounter another exile like ourselves—a pheasant, or perhaps a rabbit.

The June day of which I write was one of sweltering heat such as only the perspiring body of a great city can generate. Mutt and I had fled to Happy Home, where we wandered among the acres of gleaming headstones and imagined that each concealed the burrow of a gopher. We thought often of gophers and always with a sense of sad regret; and if we mentally populated Happy Home with the little rodents, we meant no disrespect.

After a time I heard the song of a yellow warbler in the trees beside an artificial pond, and I pursued it while Mutt, who was never much of a bird watcher, went snuffling off in the hope of finding a more interesting trail. Unexpectedly he found one and with a shrill yelp took up the chase. I turned in time to see his white rump wink out of sight among the trees.

"Rabbit—at last!" I thought and, not to be denied a glimpse of it, ran after Mutt.

When I emerged on the level burying ground beyond the pond, Mutt was already several hundred feet away. As usual his queer, lopsided gallop gave him the appearance of having a strong starboard drift, like a small sailing vessel with insufficient keel beating to weather against a stiff breeze. In point of fact Mutt was heading dead into the wind, and sailing fast and straight.

It was a light wind, but sufficient. It came gently over Mutt and on to me, and I halted in my tracks. I was a little bitter. I had so much wanted it to be a rabbit.

As I took in the scene ahead of me I saw a somber, penguinlike assembly in the distance. The sight of the funeral party shocked me into acute apprehension. I whistled frantically for Mutt, but he was deaf. Hot with the passions of his old madness, he loped resolutely on.

By this time he was rapidly approaching the funeral party from the rear, while the mourners remained all unaware. However, my whistle must have reached the ears of the undertaker's assistant, for this tall young man slowly turned about. He did not see me, for I had already resigned him to his fate and had retreated into the shelter of the willows. But he saw Mutt approaching like a dog possessed.

The skunk was a small one, probably born that spring, and it must have been distrait in those unfamiliar surroundings. Trotting nervously among the stones, it veered erratically as it attempted to decide whether Mutt or the large man in the top hat was the more formidable enemy. It was inconspicuous, and I doubt if either the undertaker's assistant or Mutt actually saw it. Mutt at least knew it was somewhere near. The assistant did not. He had begun to run toward Mutt, intending, evidently, to head him off. His mouth was working, and he looked indignant.

A Mess of Skunks

The three of them came together with perfect timing under the lee of a pink marble shaft.

It was a distressing incident, but not without some compensation, for it convinced my parents that the heart of a great city was not our chosen ground. It was directly responsible for my father's decision to move us to a village some forty miles away.

This village seemed like an odd little place to me, fresh from the untrammeled west. There was an atmosphere about it of dusty corsets, creaking whalebone, and the aggressive gentility which is assumed by so many eastern Canadian hamlets. I found myself ill at ease among the boys and girls of my own age, and I was baffled by their sober and resolute attitude of hostility. I did not understand the watchfulness of our neighbors and I could not find the means to penetrate the barrier of suspicion that surrounded us.

Our new house itself was probably much to blame for our cold reception. Its previous tenant was a sculptor, one who had little talent for his art, but who concealed this deficiency by being pugnaciously and preposterously "modernist." The house was cluttered with his experiments and we suspected that he had sold the place as the only possible means to escape from the children of his contorted ego. Most of the pieces were passionless repetitions of a nude female torso, but many others were quite inscrutable. I recall one piece in particular. It was a wood carving that resembled nothing quite so much as a bicycle wheel that had been savaged by a determined railroad locomotive. It was called *Holes in the Soul.* For some reason it irritated Mutt, and when we had banished it to the back yard, he would stand and stare at it by the hour with his teeth bared slightly in a grimace of distaste.

Nevertheless, it was not the character of the vanished sculptor that had damned the house. It was simply the fact that he was an artist, and therefore in almost any part of rural Ontario he and his domicile would have been suspect. There can be few places in the world that are so resolutely determined to defend themselves against any suspicion of culture as the villages of central Ontario. They have a steadfastness that St. Ignatius Loyola himself would have admired.

We blamed the house for the frigidity of our reception. Yet, despite its lurid past, it suited us. Its front door looked out sedately over the outskirts of a sedate community; but then the house rambled backward through sagging passages until the back door opened on an unconstrained stretch of countryside. These tangled fields were a haven, not only to Mutt and me, but to many other beasts—not least of which was a family of skunks.

We saw them almost daily, and with a special quality of resignation we awaited the inevitable; but, almost incredibly, it did not come. I do not know why this was so, except to hazard a guess that Mutt too must have felt the weight of our social isolation, and did not even have the heart for skunk conflict. There was no overt act of war, yet we remained uneasy and alert until the first heavy frosts assured us that the skunks had retreated to winter quarters.

The earth-floored basement of the house contained our winter supply of vegetables and preserves, together with a barrel of Prince Edward County apples. There was an outside cellarway, barred by a pair of massive doors, and these we closed and calked against the advent of the frost. My father and I spent a Sunday carefully sealing up the many holes in the foundation, and when we had finished hardly a mouse could have got in—or out.

We had with us at this time a maid named Hannah whom we had brought from the west. She was one of those solid, grain-fed women for which the prairies are justly famous, but she was not gifted with much brain. Nevertheless, she had a vivid, if erratic, imagination. No leap into the fantastic was beyond her, and when she noticed that the level in the apple barrel was falling with unusual rapidity, she exercised her imagination and laid a formal complaint against Mutt. It was a fascinating picture that she conjured up: Mutt, scrunched into the barrel, industriously munching apples through the long winter nights. We were almost sorry that it could not have been so.

With Mutt ruled out, Hannah was temporarily at a loss. But not for long. She was a persevering woman, and one day while we were having breakfast she startled us with a unique solution to the problem of the diminishing apple supply.

She was handing Father his plate of oatmeal, and with it she volunteered the information that:

"Them ghosts is et half all them apples up."

Father toyed delicately with the phrase for a little while, then dropped his eyes to his plate with a slight shudder. I was made of sterner stuff. "What ghosts?" I asked.

Hannah looked at me with placid condescension. "Them apple ghosts," she explained patiently. "'He's et about most of them apples you got from Prince Henry's house and just kind of lays the cores around."

After this we were driven to make a full investigation, and Hannah was relieved, yet at the same time disappointed, when I was able to tell her that we had no ghosts—only a skunk.

He was a mild-mannered fellow who must have led an unexceptional life up until the time he got himself locked up for the winter in our cellar, for there was no odor clinging to his fur. He was under the preserve cabinet when the beam of my flashlight found him. He showed no resentment, but only blinked his eyes and ducked his head in an apologetic sort of way, neither frightened nor aggressive. He must have long since assumed that we meant him no harm.

For a few days we were foolish enough to consider ways and means of removing him. Mutt, apprised of the skunk's presence, had a plan of his own and he was so anxious to put it into effect that he almost scratched a hole through the cellar door. We did not trust his discretion.

We soon recovered our reason and concluded an armistice. We had far more apples than we needed, anyway, and since the skunk was obviously amicable, we decided to live and let live.

Things worked out very well. The skunk stayed in the vegetable room, ate such apples as he required, and bothered no one. We came to accept his presence tranquilly, and it was no uncommon thing for one of us to be rummaging in the potato bin, while a few feet away the skunk munched on an apple.

This harmonious state of affairs would probably have continued until spring, when the skunk could have gone voluntarily on his way, had it not been for a man whom none of us has ever met. I do not even recall his name, but I know that he lives in one of the southern states of the Union. He is of the expert genus who write books and articles about birds and animals with such assurance that the reader is convinced the author must be privy to the thoughts of the beasts. Shortly before Christmas this man published an article about skunks in one of the more famous sporting magazines.

I read the article, and was deeply impressed. The author had developed a foolproof principle for handling skunks, and he was generous enough to share his secret with the world. The essence of his method was a garden hose. He had discovered that a jet of water directed a few inches behind a skunk, and in such a way that the stream was deflected slightly upwards after contact with the ground, would safely move any skunk that ever lived. Reasoning skunk-fashion, the author explained why the method was so effective. "The skunk," he wrote, "under the impression that his discomfort stems from a natural source, will move briskly away without attempting retaliation."

Christmas holidays were due to begin in a week's time, and I was bored and disgruntled by the last days of school. Hannah and I were alone in the house, for my parents were in Oakville on a three-day state visit to my father's family. I put down the magazine and went downstairs.

In my own defense I can plead that I was at least systematic. My first move was to pry open the outer cellar doors, and only then did I enter the basement and attach the garden hose to the laundry tap. When the hose was spluttering satisfactorily, I moved into the vegetable room and, having located the skunk, I brought the stream to bear upon the hard ground immediately to his rear.

There was a startled scurrying and the skunk shot out of the vegetable room, and sought sanctuary behind the old-fashioned hot-air furnace. I pursued him with the jet, chivying him slowly toward the cellarway and the open doors. He went, unhappily, but, even as my author had foretold, without attempt at retaliation. Victory was nearly mine, when I glanced up at the cellarway to assure myself that there was no obstacle in the skunk's way—and behold Mutt's face framed in that square of cold blue sky.

I realized that he was poised to leap, and my reason was momentarily paralyzed by a vision of the certain consequences which must follow. Acting instinctively, I raised the hose in order to bring it to bear on Mutt, but I forgot that the skunk was in the way, and the lifting stream caught him fair amidships and bowled him over. I hit Mutt too, but by then it was too late to matter much.

Tears of rage and agony were blinding me, but I no longer cared. While Mutt and the skunk skirmished around the perimeter of the basement I followed them, brandishing my hose indiscriminately. Sometimes a ricochet blast from the skunk would send me staggering back toward the cellar doors. Raging, I returned each time to the fray. Back and forth we went, into the vegetable room, behind the furnace, under the cellar stairs. The air grew murky and the single electric light bulb shone dimly through a rich and yellow haze.

A Mess of Skunks

Mutt was the first to call it quits, and to leave by the outside entrance. The skunk, exhausted and suffering from its own potency, followed close behind. I was left alone, the hose still spurting in my hand.

The silence was intense, until from somewhere far above me I heard Hannah's stentorian tones.

"Mother of God!" she cried. "Mother of God—I go!"

In the event, Hannah did not go, but only because we were so far from Saskatchewan, and she had no idea which way her lost home lay. There was no escape for any of us.

There was misery in that house for a long time. Despite the bitterness of the weather, the furnace had to be turned off, since it sucked up tangible fumes from the basement and circulated them freely. Even with all windows and doors wide to the winter winds, the basement remained a haunted place. The skunk oil, mixed with water, had permeated the dirt floor so deeply that I doubt if even yet it has entirely passed away.

As for our neighbors, far from rallying to us in this time of need, they drew yet further off. One of them was overheard to express the opinions of them all.

"What else can you expect," she said with smug complacency, "from people who would live in a place like that?" It was clear that skunks and culture were inextricably bound up together in her mind.

My parents did not punish me directly, but they insisted that I go back to school on the day after the event. I pleaded for mercy, but to no avail. I went off very slowly, and with bowed head.

[193]

The Dog Who Wouldn't Be

It was a frigid day, and the school was overheated. Before the opening exercises ended, there was not an occupied desk within five feet of me. I sat on, a self-conscious island of misery, until at last the teacher—Miss Leatherbottom was her name—called me forward and handed me a note. It was succinct. "Go home," it said.

The humiliation of that experience was a heavy load to bear, yet it was as nothing to the spiritual torment inflicted on me a few years later by Mutt and his passion for skunks.

My maternal grandparents owned a cottage and a lake in the remote highlands of Quebec, and here the family was accustomed to forgather in the summer months. It was a place of pleasant memory on the whole, for it was free of the horrors of most summer resorts. There were no thundering outboard motors piloted by fat and foolish men, hell bent at fifty miles an hour for nowhere. There were no rows of shoddy matchbox cottages clustered cheek by jowl along the shores—the sylvan counterpart of city slums. Instead there was a single unobtrusive log house, an even more unobtrusive boathouse and sleeping cabin combined, and then nothing but the ancient hills, black-shrouded in their forests, overlooking and solacing the waters of the lake.

For Mutt and me it was a blessed place after the horrors of Toronto, and the almost equal horrors of the Ontario village. It was also the scene of my first love.

The girl was the daughter of a wealthy doctor who owned a cottage on a nearby lake. She was not insensible to me, and she showed some taste for poetry, which, in those days, was my chief interest. I wrote verse of a somewhat melancholy vein, but she would listen patiently while I declaimed it. I recall one passage that seemed particularly to move her. It concerned the fate of an abandoned lover, and one verse went like this:

> Still his unseeing, dull and lidless stare
> Earnestly scans the long blue upper air;
> A corpse's gaze—save where a clinging fly
> Scuffs busily across the sunken eye.

I thought it was effective, and so did the young lady. Great things might have resulted from our association had it not been cruelly terminated within a week.

Each Saturday there was a dance in the nearby village of Kaz-abazua (you will find the name on any reputable map) and I had arranged to take my girl to one of these affairs. The explosion of a summer thunderstorm on the Friday night before the dance did not distress me as I lay abed, dreaming my dreams. Yet that storm had a shattering effect upon my life.

In its first wild rush it uprooted and toppled a magnificent old pine that had stood for two hundred years not far from the house. In its fall the old tree uncovered a family of skunks who had their burrow beneath its roots. The skunks immediately sought other shelter, and found it under the floor of the cabin where a space had been left open for ventilation purposes. Unfortunately, Mutt, whose fear of thunderstorms was still pathogenic, had long since occupied this sanctuary, and there was hardly room for all the new arrivals.

The Dog Who Wouldn't Be

My parents and grandparents were sitting by the open fire when the old tree came down. Grandmother, who always tended to take acts of God as personal affronts, was outraged. She began to pace up and down the room, peering out at the wreckage as she passed the window, and she made a little speech.

"I refuse," she cried, "absolutely refuse to plant another tree. What point is there when they just blow down again?"

Grandfather wisely let this pass, but my parents were still trying to digest it when all four of them became aware of new sounds of natural discord. From below their feet came strange and muffled scuttling noises, some snorts, a muted growl or two, and a weird sort of chattering. Grandmother, who was seldom at a loss, was mystified. She pounded the floor with her foot and cried out:

"Now what's all that about?"

The floor boards were not tight. There was no sub-floor, and Grandmother got her answer. With a callous indifference that I still find hard to forgive, my four elders promptly evacuated the house to seek shelter in the sleeping cabin by the lake. They left me to my fate.

I woke soon afterwards. The turmoil underfoot was mounting in intensity and the stench was breathtaking. Clutching an eiderdown, and burying my nose in its folds, I scuttled to the door and began slithering down the steep path to the lakeside. The thunder muttered overhead and rain drove down with a vicious intensity. A flash of lightning illuminated my path and I beheld the white and frightened face of a skunk two or three paces ahead of me, and evidently in full flight from the Donnybrook under the house.

A Mess of Skunks

I could not stop. My bare feet scratched for traction on the steep and muddy path, but it was useless. Both the skunk and I were on a greased slide, and we fetched up at the bottom of the path almost inextricably entwined with one another in the eiderdown.

They would not have me in the sleeping cabin. Grandmother held the door shut. "He's your damned dog—go and sleep with *him*," she said, and there was an unaccustomed bitterness in her tone.

As a matter of fact I slept under an upturned rowboat for the rest of the night.

At the crack of dawn on Saturday morning I was in the lake laboring with a cake of carbolic soap. At intervals during that awful day I experimented with tomato juice, kerosene, turpentine, and pumice stone, and although none of these were wholly effective, by evening I was relatively free of skunk. At least, I could no longer smell myself, and with this false assurance of purity I set out to escort my young lady to the dance.

We had no more than a few hundred yards to walk together, and there was a good evening breeze, so that by dint of remaining downwind from her, I escaped immediate detection. But she was on the alert.

"Hurry up," she said once. "I think there's a skunk somewhere about." There was something close to panic in her voice, and I was surprised by it, for she had always seemed a singularly fearless sort of girl.

The dance was in a barn and it was well attended. Oil lamps supplied the illumination, and boosted the already volcanic temperature to an almost unbearable extreme. I knew before the first dance ended that I would not get away with it. Yet by dint of refusing to sit out any dances, and by moving very quickly through the press, I kept the finger of suspicion from pointing directly at me. I was considerably relieved when, after half an hour of it, my girl clutched me by the arm and in a strangled whisper implored me to take her home at once. She kept peering at the other dancers and there was a stricken look about her.

Once out of doors I felt that I should confess my guilt. My lady had a sense of humor, and I was sure that she would be amused by the affair. We paused on the path outside her cottage, and I told her all.

She gasped, turned from me, and ran as if pursued by all the fiends of hell. And never to this day have I looked upon her face again.

It was her older brother who explained. I met him in the local general store one day and insisted that he tell me why his sister would no longer receive me.

He laughed heartily.

"You don't know?" he asked, and it was a stupid question, for how could I have known? "Oh, but this is rich! It's skunk stink," he cried when he could master his mirth. "Jane's allergic to it—it makes her break out in hives—all over—and they last a month!"

15

Afloat and Ashore

ONE of the first things my father did after we returned to Ontario to live was to give substance to a ten-year-old dream. He bought a ship. It was not a canoe this time. It was a real ship—a vessel to make any sailor proud.

She came from Montreal and she was a double-ender of a type designed originally in Norway for service on the North Atlantic, and called a *redningsskoite*. She was big, and black, and as strong and well developed as the "big-boned, deep-bosomed, buxom western women" that Father used to talk nostalgically about. She was ketch rigged. Her sails were made in Lunenburg and tanned a glowing red. Everything about her was solid and sea-going.

My father sailed her up from Montreal singlehanded, and when she arrived among the varnish and mahogany yachts of Toronto (yachts that sometimes flew streamers of ticker tape from their spars instead of pennants) she seemed as out of place as an Aberdeen Angus among a herd of fallow deer. The natty lads in their cream flannels and yachtsmen's hats were inclined to sneer at her, and when they read her name they laughed out loud.

"Scotch Bonnet!" they cried. "What kind of a name is that for a boat? Why didn't you call her *RayMar* or *Bill-Jean* or *Saucy Sue VIII* like the rest of us?"

But when they saw *our* yachting caps—Balmorals, imported direct from Caithness—they realized that we were beyond their ken entirely, and they ignored us from then on.

Scotch Bonnet did not care. She knew where her name came from, and she was proud of it. For the black granite reef that rises out of Lake Ontario below Prince Edward County, and that bears the name Scotch Bonnet Rock, is a place that once loomed large in the minds of the real sailormen who manned the grain schooners that owned the Great Lakes in the days before steam drove them into limbo.

Scotch Bonnet was—and is—a ship to inspire deep affection in her crew, and even Mutt was not immune to her attractions. He did not come to her as a complete landlubber, for he had sailed before, in *Concepcion*. Nevertheless, his first sail aboard *Scotch Bonnet* might well have turned a lesser dog against the sea forever.

In the first week of September, my father announced that he and I and Mutt would take the vessel down the lake to the Bay of Quinte. We drove from our house to the anchorage inside Toronto's breakwater, and when we arrived there we found a gale to greet us. The storm warnings were flying, and the seas, running in across some forty miles of open water, were thundering against the concrete barriers along the shore.

It was all we could do to stay afloat in our little dinghy as we rowed out to where our ship lay at her moorings; but Mutt appeared to enjoy the experience and he was full of enthusiasm as he leaped up to *Scotch Bonnet's* sturdy deck.

We had no sooner run up the mizzen, preparatory to letting slip our moorings, when a police launch came pounding out toward us. It was a big power cruiser but, like all of its species, designed for millponds. I watched in awe as it wallowed and heaved across the protected waters, and I was more than half inclined to heed the warnings shouted to us over a loud-hailer when the launch came alongside.

"Ahoy there," bawled an authoritative voice. "You can't go outside today. The gale warnings are up!"

Father, who knows how to handle policemen, simply smiled and answered them in Gaelic. The policemen were game, and they made several attempts to get through to him, but finally they took a big wave broadside and came near enough to swamping to make them decide to leave us foreigners to our fate.

Father caught sight of my face. "Buck up," he shouted over the roar of the wind. *"Scotch Bonnet's* sister ship crossed the Atlantic twice. This is only a light breeze for a *redningsskoite.* Now stand by to let slip the mooring when I get the jib up."

I stood by, but not very happily. A few moments later *Bonnet* was under way, and the water was whooshing beneath her forefoot like a mountain cascade.

We went out through the gap into the open lake under mizzen and jib alone, and it was more than enough canvas in that wind. We had no sooner cleared Toronto Island than we saw a strange spectacle ahead. It looked at first as if a drunken forest was staggering toward us out of the storm darkness. We stared perplexed at this phenomenon until my father recognized its meaning.

"Look," he whooped joyfully. "That's the cross-lake race from Rochester...the yachting boys...and they're running for shelter under bare poles."

As we stood out toward them we could see that they were certainly a naked lot. There was hardly a stitch of canvas set on any of those two dozen vessels, not even on the big eight-meter boats. They were a frightening sight, too, for they were burying their noses until the water ran green the full length of their decks, and their cockpits were no more than private swimming pools.

Father was not really a vindictive man, but I suppose he could not resist the impulse. "Take the tiller," he yelled. And with that he began hoisting our great red mainsail.

We drove through that battered fleet like another *Flying Dutchman*, and as we passed we sang "It's Up Wi' the Bonnets of Bonny Dundee" at the top of our lungs.

It was an exhilarating moment, but when we had come about and were beating eastward down the coast, I remembered that I had not seen Mutt for half an hour. I went below to seek him.

I found him on my bunk, up forward of the mainmast, where the motion was the worst. He was stretched at full length, his head on my pillow and his feet hanging limply over the side of the bunk. He looked as if he believed, and hoped, that he was already dead. He took no notice of my arrival except to roll his eyes until the sight of those bloodshot orbs made me think suddenly of my own stomach, and I hastened out on deck again.

I told my father that Mutt was dying.

"He'll get over it," my father said.

And of course he did. By the next dawn he was up and around again; but in future when the storm warnings were flying he never showed quite the same enthusiasm for sailing that had been his on that first day we went to sea.

The kind of cruising that really suited Mutt was when we lay at anchor in one or other of the many delightful little coves that hide under the high shores of Prince Edward County. He could then enjoy the best of two worlds. We used to tie the dinghy close alongside *Scotch Bonnet* and whenever Mutt felt like stretching his legs on land he had but to jump into the dinghy, lower himself over its side, and swim ashore. The coves where we chose to lie were usually remote and rather wild, and Mutt could indulge in one of his favorite sports—crawfish hunting—to his heart's content.

Crawfish hunting is an aquatic sport. To play it Mutt would wade out from shore until he stood shoulder deep. Then he would lower his head below the surface and, with his eyes wide open, would search for the flat stones under which crawfish like to hide. He used his nose to overturn the stones, and the water was so clear that he could plainly see his quarry scuttling away in search of a new haven. Being members of the lobster family, crawfish have formidable claws, but these availed them nothing against Mutt, who would snap at them with his front teeth until they were disarmed. Once they had been rendered harmless, he would take them in his mouth, raise his head out of the water, and eat them with evident relish.

Mutt, at his crawfishing, was quite a sight to see and I have known a Bay of Quinte farmer to stand and watch for a solid hour, while the plow team pawed restively at the furrowed ground behind him.

If crawfish were not abundant, or if the cove happened to be marshy, Mutt would hunt frogs instead. He did this purely for fun, since he never ate the frogs he caught. Nor would he catch a frog while it was on dry land. The trick was to chivy it into, and under, the water, and try to locate it as it huddled on the bottom. Then Mutt's head would dart down with a speed and precision equal to that of his chief competitor, the great blue heron; and generally he would emerge with the frog held gently in his jaws. He would carry it to land, release it, and then chase it back into the water, for another round.

If he grew tired of the land, or if he fell foul of a farmer as a result of his old passion for cattle chasing, Mutt had only to plunge into the cove and swim out to the dinghy again. It was a life that suited him ideally.

It was ideal for me as well, but I preferred *Scotch Bonnet* under sail, making her way in fine weather among the islands and channels of the bay. I held a bird-banding permit at the time, and the myriad islets and sand bars around Prince Edward County were densely occupied by breeding colonies of gulls and terns. *Scotch Bonnet* eventually carried me to almost all these breeding places, and I banded well over a thousand fledglings in the course of two summer cruises.

The most memorable of those banding excursions was the one we made to *Scotch Bonnet's* namesake.

Scotch Bonnet Rock lies nine miles off the Prince Edward shore, and the lighthouse that stands upon it is no longer tended by a keeper. The rock is visited only once or twice each season, when the gas cylinders of the automatic light need replenishing. Free from human interference, vast flocks of gulls and cormorants now make the rock their home and breeding place.

We came to the island from seaward on a boisterous June day, with a stiff breeze filling our sails, and a brilliant sun beating down upon the rising waves. Because of the heavy seas and the strengthening breeze, Father was forced to lie off and on under sail, beating back and forth, while I rowed ashore in the dinghy. Mutt insisted on coming with me, for we had been some time from land, and he was suffering from a lack of trees.

It was a hard pull. The sea was steep and choppy, and the little dinghy rose and fell, so that often I could see neither the island nor the vessel. But I could see the cormorants, black and heavy, in slow flight from their fishing grounds to their nests upon the island.

I landed on the lee side and hauled the dinghy clear of the swell. All about me gulls rose in angry protest, and since the wind was sweeping across the island full into my face, I was doubly aware that the place was heavily populated. Mutt dashed off to seek a tree, but there was none, and after some indecision he finally betook himself to the lighthouse, which must surely have been the most grandiose post ever to greet the eye of a hard-pressed dog.

Banding young cormorants is no job for those with weak stomachs. The fledglings are naked until they are more than half grown, and their long necks and ungainly bellies do not make for much aesthetic charm. The nests are sketchy constructions littered with fish offal and guano. When approached by one whom they suspect, the young cormorants fix the intruder with a reproachful gaze and, after letting him come within easy range, suddenly convulse themselves, regurgitating their dinners of partially digested fish at him.

Knowing of this deplorable habit, I approached my victims cautiously. Mutt, on the other hand, had no foreknowledge.

Having finished his business at the lighthouse, he began picking his way through the nesting area toward me. At first he avoided the young cormorants, but his curiosity got the better of him, and at length he approached one of them with nose outstretched in a tentative gesture of friendship. The cormorant promptly convulsed itself and caught Mutt squarely in the face.

I was roused from my work by his cry of outrage, and I stood up in time to see him come dashing blindly through the center of the colony, recklessly steering a direct course, and presenting an irresistible target to every young cormorant along the way.

He saw me and altered course in my direction, but friendship and brotherly love have their limits, and I climbed hurriedly up on a rock outcropping where I was beyond his reach. He paused briefly at the foot of the rock, fixed me with a terrible look of reproach, and then, turning to the island shore, he incontinently flung himself into the lake.

I had a hard time launching the dinghy, and by the time I was clear of the shore breakers, I could see no sign of Mutt. As the little boat clung momentarily to the top of each swell I scanned the waters. At last I caught a glimpse of his black head, and I could see that he was making directly for the mainland shore, nine miles away.

He vanished immediately from my view, but some of his erstwhile enemies from the island now came to his assistance. A bevy of gulls swooped screaming down above him, giving me an aiming mark.

Father had seen me leave the island, and he realized that all was not well. He brought the vessel about and bore down on me. I waved toward the gulls, and he understood at once, for he could see that Mutt was missing from the dinghy.

Mutt had to be dragged aboard the ship, and he showed no signs of gratitude for his rescue. The swim had cleansed his body, but the memory of the indignity he had suffered remained upon him. He crawled into a cubbyhole under the cockpit seat, and there he stayed throughout the remainder of the day and emerged— tentatively—only when we docked in the Murray Canal that evening. Even then he did not hurry ashore as was his wont, but stood on deck for a long time, suspiciously eyeing the green meadows and the inviting trees.

Mutt found long passages trying. We were never able to convince him that it was all right with us if he made use of the masts, in lieu of telephone poles. While he remained at sea he steadfastly refused to let nature take her course, either because he felt that *Scotch Bonnet* was, in effect, a house—and he was so well house-broken that he could not forget it—or because the motion of the ship made it awkward, if not impossible, for him to balance on three legs.

Consequently, when we approached our landfall after a long period at sea, Mutt would be extremely anxious to make contact. He could smell the land long before we could see it, and when he began to fidget and whine and stare longingly at the horizon, we knew that the shore would soon appear.

One summer our whole family sailed down the lake from Niagara, with Kingston as our destination, and, because of light airs, we were at sea for almost thirty-six hours. When Kingston finally hove in sight, Mutt could hardly contain himself.

Kingston was built in the earliest days of Upper Canada, and it retains much of the staid Victorianism of its heyday. Its rows upon rows of gray-stone houses reflect a kind of gray-stone mentality.

We came into the harbor, and even before we had got our lines ashore, Mutt had spanned the gap between *Scotch Bonnet* and the dock with a prodigious leap, and was away. There were no trees immediately at hand, so he raced up the old cobbled street toward the town proper.

A seedy gentleman took our lines, and after we were fast he invited himself aboard, saying that he was an old sailor—a gambit that always works on my father.

We gave him a drink, and after a while he said:

"Allow you got a dog."

We allowed that we had indeed.

"Best keep him tight aboard then," the old fellow continued. "Hear some turrible things about them young medical students up to the university. They be awful hard on dogs."

"What do they do to them?" I asked in my innocence.

The old man spat, and helped himself to another drink. "Turrible things, they do," was all that he would say.

I asked where they got the dogs and he replied that most of them came from the city pound. "I shoulda had that job—dog catcher—" he explained in an aggrieved tone, "only I'm a Liberal, and this here's a Conservative sort of place. Would have kept me good, too. Ten dollars for a dog, and five for a cat—that's what them students pay."

Father cast a slightly anxious look up the dock, but there was no sign of Mutt. "I don't suppose," he asked the old man somewhat apprehensively, "that there's any law against dogs running loose in Kingston?"

The old man snorted. "Law! Sure there's a law. Not that the feller who's dog catcher now needs no damn law. He'll snitch 'em right outa the back yard, chain and all."

Grumbling to himself, the old man left us, but before he was off the dock, we had passed him. We were in a hurry.

I went up the dock road while Father went east along the water front and Mother went west. None of the people I accosted had seen anything that answered Mutt's description, nor could I find any trace of him myself. When I returned to the dock an hour later, it was to discover that neither Father nor Mother had had any better luck.

My father began to seethe. The thought of Mutt in the toils of the local dog catcher, and perhaps already on his way to the dissection table, was enlarging his adrenal glands.

"You borrow a bicycle from the boatyard and go on looking," he told me. "I'm going to the pound."

By the time he reached the pound he had worked himself into a towering rage; but the dog catcher was not there. In his stead was an emaciated and gum-chewing youth sprawled in an old chair, reading a racing form. He listened without emotion to Father's request that Mutt be released upon the instant.

Eventually he waved a languid hand toward the wire enclosure at the rear of the building. "If your dog's there, you can have him for two bucks, mister," he said. "Say you think Red Apple has a chance in the King's Plate?"

Not trusting himself to reply, Father hurried to the enclosure, only to be confronted by an ominous lack of dogs. There was not one in the whole pound. He returned to the youth and, in a voice that raised the languid one out of his chair, demanded the dog catcher himself.

The youth grew impertinent.

"Try making like a dog then, mister," he advised. "Run out by the university. He'll pick you somewhere along the way."

If the lad had guessed how close he was to annihilation in that instant, he would have discarded the racing form forever in favor of the New Testament. It was only the fact that my father could not afford time for a diversion that saved his skin.

Outside the pound Father caught a taxi and went straight to

the city hall. He tried the mayor's office first, but that gentleman was out of town attending a conference on sewage disposal.

However, the office of the chief of police was close at hand, and Father stormed it as he might have stormed an enemy redoubt. He found no one there except a large fat constable who was unsympathetic, and inclined to quick hostility.

Very much on his dignity the constable pointed out that he did not run the "bejasusly" dog pound, and that, in any case, Father was committing a felony by allowing his dog to "run large." The librarian in my father came to the surface automatically.

"Run *at* large," he snapped.

The constable was no grammarian.

"You better run outside!" he shouted. "Or, by Hades, I'll run you in!"

Abandoning any hope of help from the civil power, Father now sought a telephone booth, and dialed the medical building at the university.

The phone rang and rang with that mechanical insistence which indicates either that no one is home or, if they are, that they are too busy to bother answering. Father suspected that they were too busy. Ghastly visions of a trussed-up Mutt being set upon by white-clad figures assailed him. He did not even wait to get his nickel back, but slammed out of the booth, for he had remembered that there was one place in Kingston where he might find aid and friends—the military barracks.

When he burst into the officer's mess he found it deserted save for the orderly officer of the day, who, by a singular coincidence, had served with Father in the Fourth Battalion during the First World War.

This officer was delighted to see an old friend; particularly so since there is nothing duller than orderly duty in a peacetime barracks. He listened with sympathy, and with a quickening gleam in his eye, as Father, having downed a quick one, poured out his story.

When the tale was told, the officer slapped Father affectionately on the shoulder, exclaiming:

"Trust the damned civilians to pull a black, eh? This is an emergency, old boy. Tell you what—we'll call out the guard and stage a proper rescue."

He was as good as his word, too, and, five minutes later, a picket of armed men was marching briskly through the city streets toward the university.

It was a lucky thing for him that the patrol did not meet the dog catcher en route, for soldiers are very fond of dogs, and they do not like the civil authority in any guise. But it was an even luckier thing that the patrol met me. Had it not done so, there might have been memorable deeds done in Kingston on that day.

I cannot believe that the students would have stood idly by while the medical building was put to the torch, and it is almost certain that the chief of police would have flung his forces into the fray on the students' side. Reinforcements would then have been required from the fort, and these might even have included the two light field-pieces (relics of the Boer War, but still capable of making dangerous noises) which stand in front of the officers' mess.

Afloat and Ashore

In a sense I am sorry that I interfered, but interfere I did. Astride my borrowed bicycle, I caught up with Father and the squad when they were still about a quarter of a mile from the university gates, and informed them that Mutt had been found.

As for Mutt, when we dragged him out from under the dock where he had been closeted with a dead white-fish for two hours past, he could not for the life of him understand my father's attitude. Mutt never did like being shouted at. He sulked for days.

16

April Passage

IT WAS raining when I woke, a warm and gentle rain that did not beat harshly on the window glass, but melted into the unresisting air so that the smell of the morning was as heavy and sweet as the breath of ruminating cows.

By the time I came down to breakfast the rain was done and the brown clouds were passing, leaving behind them a blue mesh of sky with the last cloud tendrils swaying dimly over it. I went to the back door and stood there for a moment, listening to the roundelay of horned larks on the distant fields.

It had been a dour and ugly winter, prolonging its intemperance almost until this hour, and giving way to spring with a sullen reluctance. The days had been cold and leaden and the wet winds of March had smacked of the charnel house. Now they were past. I stood on the doorstep and felt the remembered sun, heard the gibbering of the freshet, watched little deltas of yellow mud form along the gutters, and smelled the sensual essence rising from the warming soil.

Mutt came to the door behind me. I turned and looked at him

and time jumped suddenly and I saw that he was old. I put my hand on his grizzled muzzle and shook it gently.

"Spring's here, old-timer," I told him. "And who knows—perhaps the ducks have come back to the pond."

He wagged his tail once and then moved stiffly by me, his nostrils wrinkling as he tested the fleeting breeze.

The winter past had been the longest he had known. Through the short-clipped days of it he had lain dreaming by the fire. Little half-heard whimpers had stirred his drawn lips as he journeyed into time in the sole direction that remained open to him. He had dreamed the bitter days away, content to sleep.

As I sat down to breakfast I glanced out the kitchen window and I could see him moving slowly down the road toward the pond. I knew that he had gone to see about those ducks, and when the meal was done I put on my rubber boots, picked up my field glasses, and followed after.

The country road was silver with runnels of thaw water, and bronzed by the sliding ridges of the melting ruts. There was no other wanderer on that road, yet I was not alone, for his tracks went with me, each paw-print as familiar as the print of my own hand. I followed them, and I knew each thing that he had done, each move that he had made, each thought that had been his; for so it is with two who live one life together.

The tracks meandered crabwise to and fro across the road. I saw where he had come to the old TRESPASSERS FORBIDDEN sign, which had leaned against the flank of a supporting snowdrift all the winter through, but now was heeled over to a crazy angle, one jagged end tipped accusingly to the sky, where flocks of juncos bounded cleanly over and ignored its weary threat. The tracks stopped here, and I knew that he had stood for a long time, his old nose working as he untangled the identities of the many foxes, the farm dogs, and the hounds which had come this way during the winter months.

We went on then, the tracks and I, over the old corduroy and across the log bridge, to pause for a moment where a torpid garter snake had undulated slowly through the softening mud.

There Mutt had left the road and turned into the fallow fields, pausing here and there to sniff at an old cow flap, or at the collapsing burrows left by the field mice underneath the vanished snow.

So we came at last to the beech woods and passed under the red tracery of budding branches where a squirrel jabbered its defiance at the unheeding back of a horned owl, brooding somberly over her white eggs.

The pond lay near at hand. I stopped and sat on an upturned stump and let the sun beat down on me while I swept the surface of the water with my glasses. I could see no ducks, yet I knew they were there. Back in the yellow cattails old greenhead and his mate were waiting patiently for me to go so that they could resume their ponderous courtship. I smiled, knowing that they would not long be left in peace, even in their secluded place.

I waited and the first bee flew by, and little drifting whorls of mist rose from the remaining banks of snow deep in the woods. Then suddenly there was the familiar voice raised in wild yelping somewhere among the dead cattails. And then a frantic surge of wings and old green-head lifted out of the reeds, his mate behind him. They circled heavily while, unseen beneath them, Mutt plunged among the tangled reeds and knew a fragment of the ecstasy that had been his when guns had spoken over other ponds in other years.

I rose and ambled on until I found his tracks again, beyond the reeds. The trail led to the tamarack swamp and I saw where he had stopped a moment to snuffle at the still-unopened door of a chipmunk's burrow. Nearby there was a cedar tangle and the tracks went round and round beneath the boughs where a ruffed grouse had spent the night.

We crossed the clearing, Mutt and I, and here the soft black mold was churned and tossed as if by a herd of rutting deer; yet all the tracks were his. For an instant I was baffled, and then a butterfly came through the clearing on unsteady wings, and I remembered. So many times I had watched him leap, and hop, and circle after such a one, forever led and mocked by the first spring butterflies. I thought of the dignified old gentleman of yesterday who had frowned at puppies in their play.

Now the tracks led me beyond the swamp to the edge of a broad field and here they hesitated by a groundhog's hole, unused these two years past. But there was still some faint remaining odor, enough to make Mutt's bulbous muzzle wrinkle with interest, and enough to set his blunt old claws to scratching in the matted grass.

He did not tarry long. A rabbit passed and the morning breeze carried its scent. Mutt's trail veered off abruptly, careening recklessly across the soft and yielding furrows of October's plow, slipping and sliding in the frost-slimed troughs. I followed more sedately until the tracks halted abruptly against a bramble patch. He had not stopped in time. The thorns still held a tuft or two of his proud plumes.

And then there must have been a new scent on the wind. His tracks moved off in a straight line toward the country road, and the farms which lie beyond it. There was a new mood on him, the ultimate spring mood. I knew it. I even knew the name of the little collie bitch who lived in the first farm. I wished him luck.

I returned directly to the road, and my boots were sucking in the mud when a truck came howling along toward me, and passed in a shower of muddy water. I glanced angrily after it, for the driver had almost hit me in his blind rush. As I watched, it swerved sharply to make the bend in the road and vanished from my view. I heard the sudden shrilling of brakes, then the roar of an accelerating motor—and it was gone.

I did not know that, in its passing, it had made an end to the best years that I had lived.

In the evening of that day I drove out along the road in company with a silent farmer who had come to fetch me. We stopped beyond the bend, and found him in the roadside ditch. The tracks that I had followed ended here, nor would they ever lead my heart again.

It rained that night and by the next dawn even the tracks were gone, save by the cedar swamp where a few little puddles dried quickly in the rising sun. There was nothing else, save that from a tangle of rustling brambles some tufts of fine white hair shredded quietly away in the early breeze and drifted down to lie among the leaves.

The pact of timelessness between the two of us was ended, and I went from him into the darkening tunnel of the years.

THE END

NONPAREIL BOOKS *returns to print important and enjoyable books that we feel are a vital contribution to literature. All* NONPAREILS *are printed on acid-free paper in permanent softcover editions, designed for years of use and made to last.*

NB: *The* ISBN *prefix for titles with an asterisk is 1-56792.
The prefix for all others is 0-87923.*

NONPAREIL BOOKS are available in finer bookstores. If your bookstore does not carry a particular title, you may order it directly from the publisher by calling 1-800-344-4771, or by sending prepayment for the price of the books desired, plus $5 postage and handling, to:

DAVID R. GODINE, PUBLISHER · Box 450 · Jaffrey, New Hampshire 03452.